SACRED SYMBOLS THAT SPEAK

A study of the symbols used in the Orthodox Church

Vol. I

by

Anthony M. Coniaris

"In Him was life and the life was the light of men" (John 1:4).

Light and Life Publishing Company
P.O. Box 26421
Minneapolis, Minnesota 55426

Light and Life Publishing Company
P.O. Box 26421
Minneapolis, Minnesota 55426-0421

Copyright © 1985
Anthony M. Coniaris
Library of Congress Card No. 85-050295

All rights reserved. No part of this book may be reproduced, stored in a retrieval system, or transmitted in any form or by any means, electronic, mechanical, photocopying, recording, or otherwise, without the written permission of Light and Life Publishing Company.

ISBN 0-937032-39-5

Dedicated
to my spiritual Father, Archbishop Iakovos, Greek Orthodox Primate of North and South America, on the occasion of his fiftieth year in the priesthood.

Acknowledgements
Our deep appreciation to Father John Matusiak for the art work used in this volume.

Foreword

Someone once noted that we are radically symbol-making beings. Symbols are made from words, things or actions. They lead to the knowledge of something other than themselves. They refer to realities beyond themselves.

Symbols are dynamic forms of expression that engage the heart and grasp the imagination. They speak to the mind, spirit and intuition. They are the language by which inward and invisible realities are revealed and the core meanings of life find expression.

Symbols can help us to sense truth, beauty, goodness and holiness. They are visual homilies; a canvass of a million words compacted gently into a single phrase, or a simple gesture, or a commonplace thing.

Symbols are a powerful system of communication. They transmit ideas and feelings, and synthesize the ethos and world view of a community. Some symbols are recognizable by all, while others are familiar to persons of a particular cultural, religious or linguistic group.

The twelve chapters of this delightful book by Father Anthony Coniaris tell the story of the symbols through which Orthodox Christians celebrate their faith in the Triune God.

Weaving together effective illustrations, numerable quotations, charming verse and attractive, clear prose, Father Coniaris brings to light and life the symbols of the Orthodox Church and examines their mystical and spiritual meaning. By looking at divine truth through the network of the Church's symbols, the author allows the reader to recognize God's loving presence in all creation and to appreciate the richness of Orthodoxy's liturgical ethos.

†Alkiviadis C. Calivas, Priest

Table of Contents

                                                                 Page

Chapter 1
  Symbols - What Are They?   1

Chapter 2
  Incense: We Are the Aroma of Christ to God . 15

Chapter 3
  Candles: The Inner and the Outer Flame 27

Chapter 4
  The Flowering of the Cross:
    The Cross and Flowers 47

Chapter 5
  The Ladder to Heaven 61

Chapter 6
  Hesychasm: The Practice of Silence 77

Chapter 7
  Palms: Symbols of Victory, Surrender,
    and Allegiance 93

Chapter 8
  Good Friday: The Epitaphion
    and the Tomb of Jesus 103

Chapter 9
  The Theotokos With Child in the Apse:
    "Until Christ Be Formed In You" 125

Chapter 10
  Christ Pantocrator 137

Chapter 11
  The Divine Liturgy: Reality Not Symbol 155

Chapter 12
  Epiphany and the Blessing of Water 195

Chapter 1

Symbols - What Are They?

When asked to name a personal possession that had given her the most value for the money, the noted humorist Erma Bombeck replied:

> *"I would have to say this about my wedding ring. For years it has done its job. It has led me not into temptation. It has reminded my husband numerous times at parties that it's time to go home. It has been a source of relief to a dinner companion. It has been a status symbol in the maternity ward. It has reminded me every day of the last 30 years that I have someone who loves me."*

Autos as Symbols

Symbols play an important role in advertising, especially when it come to automobiles. Most people do not purchase an auto on the basis of its good engine but for psychological reasons. The car fulfills an inner need for power, for macho. Thus the car becomes a symbol that tells us much about the person who drives it. Some older drivers, for example, actually fear and stay out of the way of sleek sports cars. For them such a car is a symbol of reckless speed.

The Almighty is in the Dollar

A rare coin dealer pointed out once how much of the Almighty is in the "almighty" dollar. If you would take out a dollar bill and look at it, you will observe the following points. There are two circles representing both sides of the Great Seal of the United States. Thomas Jefferson, Benjamin Franklin and John Adams spent six years designing the seal which was approved by Congress on June 20, 1782. The pyramid in the left circle represents material strength and endurance. Its unfinished top signifies that there's more work to be done. The all-seeing "Eye of God" on top of the pyramid emphasized the reign and supremacy of God over the material things in the universe. He comes first; material things second. The Founding Fathers thus expressed their faith that our strength is rooted in God, and all that we do with our money and life is under His watchful eye.

The words *Annuit Coeptis* that circle the top of the seal mean, "God has favored our undertaking." The other three Latin words under the pyramid, "Novus Ordo Seclorum," meaning "a new order of things," express the freedom of the American people to practice self-government. The Roman numerals at the base of the pyramid remind us of our nation's birth date: 1776.

If you will now look at the right hand circle you will see the eagle, a symbol of strength and victory, which was selected as our national symbol in 1782. The shield on its breast signifies self-reliance and contains thirteen stripes for the thirteen states. It holds an olive branch on one talon with thirteen leaves, symbolizing peace. On its other talon it holds a bundle of thirteen arrows, symbolizing protection and power. Above the eagle's head is a ring of light surrounding thirteen stars. This symbolizes a new nation taking its place among the sovereign powers of the world. Thus, we see that the "almighty" dollar actually does have a lot of the Almighty God in it. It is a beautiful symbol of what this great nation stands for. The words "In God We Trust" are not empty words. Our nation has been founded on them. All of this is represented on the dollar bill which turns out to be quite a powerful symbol of what America stands for.

Saying Hello to God

Glen Kittler tells the following charming story concerning the practice of tipping one's hat as one passes a church.

"While I was going to college, I had a summer job in a Chicago bank where I became close friends with one of my co-workers. He was Protestant and I was Catholic.

One day as we were traveling by bus to his home for dinner, we passed a large church.

'Watch all the Catholic men in the bus tip their hats,' I whispered to him.

Sure enough, as the bus rumbled past the church, people throughout the bus tipped their hats. Some of them without even looking up from their newspapers.

My Protestant friend asked, 'Why do they do that?'

I answered, 'It's just a way of saying hello to God.'

After we reached our stop, we had a few blocks to walk before coming to my friend's house. As we approached a church, my friend pointed toward it and said, 'Here's where I go to church. Do we say hello?'

'Of course we do,' I replied—and we tipped our hats.

In the same block there was a building that, judging from the Star of David on the door, was a synagogue. Neither my friend or I said a word. We simply tipped our hats."

Tipping one's hat as one passes a house of worship is a reverent and beautiful symbol of one's devotion and respect for God.

The Auca Indians

Some years ago the Auca Indians in South America killed five American missionaries who had landed in their midst to preach the Gospel. They landed on a sand strip and tried to show the Indians in every way they knew that they were friendly. One of the missionaries put his arm around an Auca man, a gesture which to a Westerner cannot be understood in any other way than friendliness. Years later it was learned from the Aucas themselves that they had taken this to be proof of the foreigner's being a cannibal. What to us was a symbol of friendship, to them was a symbol of cannibalism and resulted in the killing of five missionaries. If they had known the deadly meaning to the Aucas of that innocent symbol, it would have saved their lives. Symbols! Who can deny their importance?

Solzhenitsyn writes about the old domed churches that everywhere dot the countryside in the Soviet Union. They stand, he says, as beautiful symbols of God's presence in an officially Godless nation that treats its men and women like animals.

What is A Symbol

Symbols! What are they?

The word symbol is derived from two Greek words *syn* and *balo* which means to bring two realities together and place them side by side.

Leonid Ouspensky, that brilliant expositor of the Orthodox language of symbolism, holds that it is necessary for us to distinguish between *sign* and *symbol:* "The sign limits itself to a particular fact," he writes, "the symbol expresses and somehow incorporates and makes present a higher reality. To understand a symbol is to experience a presence; to understand a sign is to translate a piece of information. Let us take the cross as an example. In arithmetic it is simply a sign which denotes addition. In the Highway Code it indicates a crossroads. But in religion it is a symbol which expresses and communicates the inexhaustible content of the Christian faith. Symbolism plays a very important role in the Church, because everything in the Church has, so to speak, a dual character: material and spiritual. The material is directly accessible to our senses; the spiritual is suggested to us through symbols."[1]

Avery Dulles defines a symbol as "an externally perceived sign that works mysteriously on the human consciousness so as to suggest more than it can clearly describe or define. . . . The symbol is a sign pregnant with a depth of meaning which is evoked rather than explicitly stated."[2]

Reveal and Conceal

Even so, symbols reveal at the same time as they hide. In the words of Leonid Ouspensky, "Symbolism, the language of mystery, reveals the truth to those who know how to interpret it, while concealing it from the uninitiated."[2] Thus, symbols both reveal and conceal. They never completely capture the reality which they seek to express. There is always something left unsaid. This allows symbols to serve as the proper language for what Orthodox theology calls "mystery."

Through symbols God penetrates created things and reveals Himself to us through the channels of sense. As someone so well said, "All symbols function together in a trinitarian way, singing the thrice-holy hymn in their concretely expressive language."

The Need for Symbols

Why do we need symbols?

Reporters once asked the famous choreographer, Martha Graham, "What does your dance mean?" She replied, "Darlings, if I could tell you, I would not have danced it." It has been said that the loftiest truths can only be communicated through symbols. As man cannot live by bread alone, so he cannot live by word alone. Something more than words is needed to help express the inexpressible.

The Orthodox Church has always used visible things to help make known to us the invisible realities that are beyond the reach of our senses. For, as St. John of Damascus says, "We are not able to bring ourselves to contemplate spiritual things without some intermediary, and in order to do this we need something close and familiar."

Symbols are carriers of meaning and tradition that speak to the whole person because they speak through the senses. We shall not need images and symbols in the kingdom, for then we shall see God face to face. But in the world where "we see in a glass darkly," symbols transmit rays of light that help penetrate the darkness.

Iconoclasm Today

Margaret R. Miles of the Harvard Divinity School wants Protestants and others to recover the importance of images and symbols in worship. Their iconoclasm, she feels, went too far, especially for an age in which people think in terms of the visual and have only secular images on which to concentrate.

In the absence of religious symbols, she says, the secular symbols have taken over and are controlling our values and attitudes. She writes, "*Theoria*, contemplation in which one is lifted out of one's familiar world and into the living presence of the spiritual world, begins with *physical* vision, with a trained and focused seeing that overcomes barriers between the visible and the spiritual world. Moreover, contemplation forms community. . . We need, says someone named Arnheim, to 'understand through the eyes'" (Harvard Divinity School Bulletin).

Speaking to the issue of how some Protestant Christians abrogated the use of symbols, Weldon Hardenbrook, an Orthodox Evangelical, writes, "Even Martin Luther, who is called the Father of the Protestant Reformation, called on his flock to use the sign of the cross. . . . It was not until the Sixteenth Century, at the time of King James, that a small group of Puritans began writing and speaking against the use of the sign of the cross. . . . Today, many American Christians have been deceived . . . into being ashamed of embracing the glory of the cross upon their breast. But hungry for a way to physically express their allegiance to Christ, many of those who reject making the sign of the cross have ended up creating their own Christian hand signs."

He goes on to explain how the "Jesus Movement" invented the "one way" sign to express that Jesus is the only way to God. This sign consisted of the index finger pointing upward. But the sign did not last, he writes. "It wasn't orthodox; it wasn't the Church's sign. It wasn't the sign of the cross. The cross is not novel; it is the true sign that belongs to each Christian."[3]

———— Symbols Communicate Powerfully ————

The smile of one small child tells more about joy than a whole book. The tears of a family by a graveside express grief in a way that frustrates words, however eloquent. The sight of a person on his knees speaks of faith in its fullness, beyond efforts to define.

A smile, a tear, a bodily posture, a photograph: each in its own way communicates immediately, powerfully, sensitively, significantly. Each is a symbol that is easily understandable, invested with the power to break through the barriers of language and abstraction and to communicate a greater reality. Mircea Eliade, chairman of the Department of History of Religions at the University of Chicago, writes in his book "The Sacred and the Profane" (Harvest Book): ". . . symbolism plays a decisive part in the religious history of humanity; it is through symbols that the world becomes transparent, is able to show the transcendent."

The Orthodox Church makes extensive use of symbols. Fr. George Maloney has written:

> *"Symbols are man's signposts that lead him into communication with the Divine. They are metarational signs of an interior world that is very real, but whose existence will always remain unknown unless human beings learn the importance of religious symbols. Carl G. Jung has pointed out that the impoverished West has lost the ability to live with myths and symbols. . . . From Eastern Christianity there is a new-felt influence upon Western Christians through the beautiful Byzantine icons, the Jesus Prayer and the haunting Liturgies so full of hieratic symbols that lead a worshiper into a deep experience of God through vivid sense impressions. . . ."* [4]

Beethoven's "Moonlight Sonata"

An example of how symbols help express what simple words cannot is an incident taken from the life of Beethoven. He had a friend, a baroness, who was desolate from the death of her only child. Beethoven was so close to the family that he felt the loss personally and shared it as his own. When he visited his friend after the funeral, he could find no word of comfort to speak for he had no word of comfort to say. He went to the piano and started to play a melody we now know as "The Moonlight Sonata." Even in the darkest night, he was trying to express the thought that there is harmony and life if we are sensitive enough to appreciate and hear. Afterward the baroness said, "He told me everything I needed to know."

What could not be expressed with words was expressed through music.

Radical Christian Materialists

Dr. Anthony Ugolnik has written,

> *"The Orthodox could better be understood . . . as radical Christian materialists. We perceive God as immanent in His Creation, as inherent in the material*

world; our symbolism continually calls that immanence to mind. . . . For all our mysticism, we Orthodox are shockingly 'material,' as many of our Puritan detractors have noted, in our expression of faith. We engage all the senses in worship. With the sacraments as our model, we continually draw a connection between a given 'thing' and what it 'signifies.' . . . Thinkers like the religious philosopher Vladimir Solovyev can see the whole of the material world as charged with Divinity, with Christ as the Ultimate Theophany in a series of theophanies. This Christ is the fullest expression of God's immanence in His Creation. . . . Our rites of observance—veneration of icons, vigil lights, blessings—these liberate material objects from secular autonomy and restore their relationship within the scheme of Creation. . . . We take the Christian artist absolutely seriously as a theologian. The iconographer, the musician, the poet and hymnographer, and no less the novelist—each of these manipulates a material medium, sanctifies it, and restores it to his or her God." [5]

On Dis-Incarnating Christianity

The Greek Orthodox theologian, Dr. Nikos Nissiotis, clarifies the use of symbols in the Orthodox Church:

"Ikons and liturgical gestures and actions are a legitimate use of nature which in an eschatological perspective is already restored, in order that the worshipping community may receive the real presence of the Lord coming in His Glory. None of these symbolic elements is an end in itself. None is presented as a sine qua non condition. Matter and colours and movements and the set forms of an ecclesiastical life are transparent facades set forth in front of the eyes of the faithful by which to look through to the hidden spiritual realities of the celestial world. There is, therefore, no question of the worship of Ikons or of a superstitious reverence for sacred objects, but rather of respect for every object which is used by the pray-

ing community as material selected out of the Creation of God, in order to render His glory more immediately present around the eucharist which is thus seen as the omnipotent centre of all worship.

"The absence of symbolism in Christian worship is not simply an absence of a secondary item in the Christian life; rather it denotes a dangerous inclination to dis-incarnate the whole content of Christian faith and to arrive at a kind of spiritualistic monism. One must see the Orthodox community as grounded precisely on this 'materialism' of worship, and blended in and with this saved world. A worshipping community prays and offers not only its own gifts, and its own prayer, but the whole creation and the whole world with all its problems, though in a doxological and hymnological way." [6]

Leonid Ouspensky adds: ". . . in the primitive churches, just as in ours today, everything has a symbolic meaning, everything was designed to lift up the soul and spirit of man to the divine life. In other words, the very architecture of the churches, lifts us up to contemplate realities which are not only invisible but which also cannot be expressed directly. The objects that our bodily eyes behold thus become symbols which introduce us to the divine world. This is an application of the patristic formula: visible objects lift us up to the contemplation of invisible things." [7]

Purpose of Symbols

Fr. Thomas Hopko describes the purpose of symbols when he writes:

This, after all, is what Thomas Merton's 'gold-encrusted cult thick with the smoke of incense and populated with a legion of gleaming icons' is all about. It manifests the fact that God is with us and we are with Him, with all of the angels and saints and the whole of creation, in a 'kingdom which cannot be shaken.' Everything in the Church—not only the icons and the incense, but also the songs and the hymns, the dogmas and the prayers, the vestments and the candles, the processions and the prostrations—bears wit-

ness to the fact that the Church is salvation: communion with God in His redeemed, resurrected, transfigured and glorified creation. Everything proclaims the fact that the Messiah has come, that God is with us, and that all things have been made new. Everything cries out with the fact that 'through Him we have access in one Spirit to the Father' and are 'no longer strangers and sojourners, but . . . fellow citizens with the saints and members of the household of God . . . Christ Jesus Himself being the cornerstone, in whom the whole structure is joined together, and grows into a holy temple in the Lord . . . a dwelling place of God in the Spirit' (Eph. 2:18-22).[8]

We must realize that Christianity is a personal encounter with the living Christ and not merely with the symbols of the Church. Symbols are means toward this goal. Only as long as they contribute toward this goal are symbols valid. Christians used symbols from the beginning. They employed such symbols as the Peacock (symbol of the resurrection), the Dove (symbol of the peace of Christ), the Fish and the Shepherd (symbols of Christ).

Symbols and Children

In the Orthodox Church children first experience the faith through its art and symbols. From the earliest years the child is exposed to the same symbols as the adults are. There are no children's liturgies, for example. The child begins to be introduced to God early through the senses by kissing the icons, saying the Jesus Prayer, etc. These are the same symbols as the adults use, so the child does not have to outgrow them at a later date. As Sophie Koulomzin writes, "In our Church all these physical objects, sensations and experiences are not merely religious baby-talk to be discarded later. Each of the things . . . remains a perfectly valid, meaningful action, gesture or experience throughout an Orthodox Christian's life."

As the child grows it will want to know what these symbols mean. It will ask questions about them which will give parents the opportunity to share their faith with their children. Joshua, for example, placed twelve stones at the ford where his army crossed the Jordan River, noting that future generations would ask, "What do these stones mean?'' The question would give an opportunity to tell of the victory of their people. Thus, the symbols of the Church serve as powerful tools for educating our children in the faith.

Nikos Kazantzakis, author of "Zorba the Greek" wrote, "The Word, in order to touch me, must become flesh. Only then do I understand—when I can smell, see and touch." This is exactly what religious symbols help us do. The Word, the faith, must be made tangible and palpable if our children are to know it in their hearts as well as in their heads.

Symbols in the Bible

The use of symbols is scriptural. More than once the prophets resorted to symbolic actions when they felt that words were not enough to convey their message. That is what Jeremiah did when he made bonds and yokes and wore them to express the coming servitude of the Jews (Jeremiah 27). That is what Jesus did when He introduced the Eucharist during the Jewish Passover meal and said to His disciples, "Look! Just as this bread is broken, my body will be broken for you. Just as this cup of wine is poured out, so my blood will be poured out for your salvation." The meal which commemorated liberation from the slavery of Egypt was chosen by Jesus to introduce the Eucharist through which the blood of the Lamb of God—Jesus—would be given to us through the ages, not in a symbolic but in a real way, to liberate us from slavery to sin and death.

The Book of Revelation is replete with symbols. The harlot Babylon is pagan Rome. The woman pursued into the desert is the Church. The beast whose number is 666 is Nero. The plagues suggest that like the slaves in the Exodus, the new people of Israel can look forward to deliverance. The rich use of symbolism in the Orthodox Church is anchored in Scripture. That is perhaps why Rheinhold Neihbur said once, "It is the task of theologians to interpret symbols."

Symbols Shape Us

Sir Winston Churchill said once that we first shape buildings and then they shape us. So it is with symbols. The Bible and the Church have shaped symbols for us and then they in turn shape us. As Father John of Kronstadt wrote:

The Church, through the ordering of the church building and her divine service, acts upon the whole man, educates him wholly; acts upon his sight, hearing, smelling, feeling, taste, imagining, mind and will, by the splendor of the images, and of the building in general, by the fragrance of the incense, by the veneration of the gospels, cross and images, by the singing, and by the reading of the scriptures.[9]

Be a Symbol

St. Peter's Cathedral in Rome stands on the site of Nero's Circus, a stadium where public shows were put on by the emperor, including the martyrdom of many Christians. In that arena stood an obelisk, a monumental shaft of stone brought from Egypt. That shaft now stands in the center of St. Peter's Square, and surmounting the monument is a cross, symbolic of the fact that the might of the Roman Empire lost out to the power of the Christian faith.

Christianity won because the Christians, as has been truly said, out-thought, out-lived, and out-died their pagan contemporaries. Their strong commitment was based on faith that God would be with them in life, in death, and beyond—so there was nothing to fear.

The ultimate is not just to have symbols but to *be* a symbol. And those early Christians became, by God's grace, symbols of God's presence in the world. They were light, salt and yeast for Christ. By God's grace and through His presence in us each one of us can be a living symbol glorifying the Father, the Son and the Holy Spirit. Amen.

> "*He who once spoke through symbols to Moses on Mt. Sinai,*
> *Saying, 'I am who is,'*
> *Was transfigured today upon Mount Tabor before the disciples;*
> *And in his own person he showed them the nature of man,*
> *Arrayed in the original beauty of the image.*
> *Having gone up the mountain, O Christ, with thy disciples,*

*Transfigured thou hast made our human nature,
Grown dark in Adam, to shine again as lightning,
Transforming it into the glory and splendour of
 thine own divinity.''*
Orthodox Hymn—Transfiguration

Chapter 2

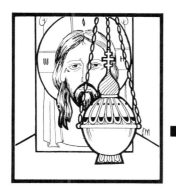

Incense: We Are the Aroma of Christ to God
(II Corinthians 2:15)

Someone said once that incense does for the Orthodox in their weekly worship what organ music does for the Protestants: it lifts them over the threshold of the church.

It is not man alone who glorifies God with incense; nature has always done so. Beverly Nichols has written:

"Every moment of this strange and lovely life, from dawn to dusk, is a miracle. Somewhere, always, a rose is opening its petals to the dawn. Somewhere, always, a flower is fading in the dusk. The incense that rises with the sun, and the scents that die in the dark, are all gathered, sooner or later, into the solitary fragrance that is God. Faintly, elusively, that fragrance lingers over all of us."

The Oldest Silent Language in the World

Science tells us that all around us the air is filled with subtle odors that, like sacred signals, communicate a variety of messages. It is the oldest silent language in the world.

Most living things still use the sense of smell to communicate. For example, when your pet cat greets you by rubbing her cheek against your leg, it has scent glands near the base of its whiskers, and is marking you with a scent that says to other cats, "This human is my property." Dogs, of course, do the same.

Scientists are now discovering special odors that reduce anxiety and stress in workers. They believe that the right odors may increase efficiency in factories and offices, and even reduce levels of aggression and violence in prisons.

We know, of course, that in ancient times doctors diagnosed illnesses by how their patients smelled. Typhoid fever was said to produce a smell like hot bread, measles like freshly plucked feathers, insanity like the scent of mice or deer, plague like honey, yellow fever like a butcher-shop odor. Odors are indeed the silent language still used by most of the world to communicate.

_____ Every Church Should Have a Fragrance _____

One authority states that cities have an odor all their own—Pittsburgh smells of steel, Hershey of chocolate, South Chicago of soap.

Churches also have an odor all their own. Some are so stuffy that it is almost impossible to do anything but sleep in them. Others smell musty, for the fresh air seldom gets in. Others have a funeral atmosphere, as if the dead lay constantly in the shadows. Others are cold and chilly.

What a joy it is to get into a fresh, sweet-smelling church. After all, a church should have a fragrance about it that attracts people to it. It should have quiet, to purify the mind and strengthen the soul. It should have peace, which reinforces troubled minds. It should have strength to bring healing to the spiritually ill. It should have pungent activity, to lift children and youth. It should have the fragrance of flowers, to recall long-forgotten things of joy and beauty. Indeed, every church should radiate the fragrance of Christ. "We are the aroma of Christ to God," says St. Paul.

It is not strange then that incense has been used from time immemorial by many religions in the world to communicate important messages in worship. Let us see how this was done and what message is conveyed in worship today through incense.

Noah Offers Incense To God

When Noah came out of the ark to find himself and his family saved from the flood which had destroyed the rest of the world, he did something to thank God:

> *"Then Noah built an altar to the Lord, and took of every clean animal and of every clean bird, and offered burnt offerings on the altar. And when the Lord smelled the pleasing odor, the Lord said in his heart, 'I will never again curse the ground because of man.'"* *(Gen. 8:20-21).*

After the flood had receded, Noah did not just say, "Thank you, Lord!"; He did something to thank Him. He prepared a burnt offering whose fragrance reached all the way up to heaven. The fragrant smoke ascending to heaven symbolized Noah's prayers of thanksgiving rising up to God.

Zechariah and the Angel

We need to remember that every morning and evening in the Old Testament temple, a sacrifice was made for the whole nation. A male lamb, without spot or wrinkle, one year old, was offered in sacrifice. Before the morning sacrifice and after the evening sacrifice incense was burned at the altar of incense. The censing of the altar morning and evening expressed the desire of the people that the sacrifices may go up to God wrapped in an envelope of sweetness and thus be acceptable to Him.

When God gave Moses instructions for the tabernacle that was built in the wilderness, he was told to build an altar of incense immediately before the Holy of Holies. An offering of incense was to burn continually on the coals of fire. Thus, the altar had a continual fire with incense burning upon it, and there were regular times during the day when it was specifically attended. The continually rising smoke symbolized the prayers of God's people rising to heaven (Rev. 5:8-9).

It was the custom in the Old Testament for one priest to be selected by lot each day to enter the ante-chamber of the Holy of Holies in the Temple where he would offer incense to God. We read in Luke 1:8-23 that one day Zechariah, the husband of Elizabeth and the father of John the Baptist, who was a priest, was selected by lot to enter the ante-chamber to the Holy of Holies and offer incense to God. Holding his censer high, he began to mount the twelve steps, one for each of the tribes of Israel. Lifting the temple veil with his left hand, he disappeared into the tabernacle, where minor priests came closest to the presence of God. There was not much for Zechariah to do in the chamber of incense. He was to stand only for a moment in silent prayer. He was to look up at the golden candlesticks and down upon the cakes made of wheat and barley with oil of honey. Then, looking upon the twelve loaves of showbread in a prolonged moment of silence, he was supposed to swing the censer three times. After which he was to back out of the holy place, face the reverent multitude, and offer up the final prayer of blessing.

But you recall that something happened that day to Zechariah as he was offering incense to God. "There appeared to him an angel of the Lord standing on the right side of the altar of incense. And Zechariah was troubled when he saw him and fear fell upon him. But the angel said to him, 'Do not be afraid, Zechariah, for your prayer is heard, and your wife Elizabeth will bear you a son, and you shall call his name John'" (Luke 1:11-13). Commenting on this incident, St. Ambrose said, "Would that an angel would stand by us also whenever we cense the altar and offer our sacrifices."

The Angel of the Apocalypse

In the Book of Revelation we read, "And another angel came and stood at the altar with a golden censer; and he was given much incense to mingle with the prayers of all the saints upon the golden altar before the throne; and the smoke of the incense rose with the prayers of the saints from the hand of the angel before God" (Rev. 8:3-4). "Here we see that the incense represents the prayers of the saints—both those in heaven and those on earth—rising up to God as a fragrant offering of thanksgiving, as they sing a new song, 'Worthy is the Lamb.'"

The Fragrance of Mary's Anointing

The offering of incense is much like Mary's anointing of Jesus at Bethany. She poured an expensive perfume—worth a whole year's salary—on the feet of Jesus and wiped them with her hair. The whole house was filled with the fragrance of the ointment. Judas objected, "Why this waste?" Jesus replied, "Let her alone. She is preparing my body for burial."

Romano Guardini has written,

> *"The offering of incense is like Mary's anointing at Bethany. . . . It is the offering of a sweet savour which Scripture itself tells us is the prayer of the Saints. Incense is a symbol of prayer. . . . It rises like the Gloria at the end of a psalm in adoration and thanksgiving to God for His great glory. . . . It rises like beauty, like sweetness, like love."* [10]

___ Clouds of Incense Symbolizing God's Presence ___

When the Temple in Jerusalem was being dedicated, the glory of God descended upon the Holy of Holies in the form of a cloud (3 Kings 8:10-11). At the transfiguration, again, a cloud overshadowed Jesus. The voice of God spoke from the cloud saying, "This is my beloved Son; listen to Him." In Old Testament thought, the presence of God is regularly connected with a cloud. It was in the cloud that Moses met God. It was through a cloud that God filled the Temple when it was dedicated after Solomon built it. And it was the dream of the Jews that when the Messiah came, the cloud of God's presence would return to the Temple. St. Symeon of Salonika suggests that this is why the priest censes the entire church before the liturgy, vespers and other services. The clouds of incense filling the sanctuary suggest the glory of God descending upon those who come to worship Him. He writes, "Like a cloud also the incense is offered, symbolizing the Holy Spirit and the transmission of His divine grace and fragrance."

_____ A Pinch of Incense to Caesar _____

In the Roman Empire all subjects were required to appear before a statue of Caesar yearly, throw a pinch of incense into the fire that burned before it, and say, "Caesar is Lord." Because the early Christians refused to do this, they were thrown to the lions. It was unthinkable for them to confess publicly someone other than

Jesus as their true God. The pinch of incense for them meant a betrayal of Jesus.

I remember seeing a television film in which a group of Christians was huddled together in a dungeon beneath the Colosseum in Rome. They were to be thrown to the lions the next day. The Roman commander had fallen in love with a beautiful Christian girl and wanted to marry her. He tried to persuade his beloved to save herself from the lions by meeting the simple requirement of the Roman Government and putting a pinch of incense in the altar fire before the statue of Caesar. She refused.

"But it's such a little thing," he said. "Why should you die for being so stubborn? You don't have to give up any of your beliefs or take on any new ones. We don't ask you to stop being a Christian. All you have to do is just this little thing, so that the Government can know that you are a loyal subject. Then you and I can get married and live in peace. Is a pinch of incense so great a sacrifice for life, love and happiness?" Though she loved him, this young Christian girl refused to throw that pinch of incense into the fire. She had only one Lord and he was not Caesar.

A pinch of incense thrown into the fire meant acknowledging someone as god. Christians would burn incense before no one but the one, true Lord. This is one reason we continue to use incense in our worship today. Whenever I throw a "pinch of incense" into my censer at home before the icon of Jesus; whenever as a priest I cense the icon of Jesus in church, I am acknowledging Him to be my Lord and God.

The Meaning of Incense

The meaning of incense is rich and varied. It means the prayers of the saints ascending to God. "Let my prayer rise like incense before you, my hands like the evening sacrifice" we sing in the vesperal psalm (Ps. 140:2). Incense denotes the fragrance of prayer to God. Burning incense before Jesus is a public confession of faith in Him as our true Lord. The rising smoke of the incense calls on us to seek constantly the things that are above, where Jesus is seated at the right hand of God. It raises our sights from earth to heaven.

The offering of incense in vespers accompanies Psalm 140 and has a penitential meaning: It is a symbol of our self-offering, of repentance rising with our prayers and our uplifted hands.

The clouds of incense symbolize the glory of God that is present as we worship Him. When the priest turns from censing the saints to cense each worshiper in the congregation, he is paying homage and respect to the image of God in each one of us. He reminds us of our high calling to theosis whereby we are invited to rise to where God is, becoming partakers of divine nature. In the words of Fr. John of Kronstadt, "The fragrance of incense reminds us by analogy of the fragrance of virtue, and by contrast of the evil odour of sins, and teaches those who are attentive to inward feelings to avoid the stench of vices . . . and adorn themselves with every Christian virtue."[11] As a prayer from the ancient liturgy of St. James says, "Receive from us your unworthy servants, O Lord, this incense for a fragrant sacrifice, and make fragrant the stench of our soul and body."

During the funeral service we cense the body of the deceased to pay respect to the temple of the Holy Spirit which God will one day bring back to life.

It is interesting that St. Demetrios is called *Myrovlitis* in Greek in view of the fact that the place where he was buried in Thessalonika emitted a fragrance. Other saints whose relics emit the fragrance of holiness are also given the name *Myrovlitis,* i.e., "emitting a fragrant odor." It is said of the martyrdom of St. Polycarp that his burning body emitted "a fragrant scent like incense or other costly spices."

Incense reminds us that God is pleased not just with fragrant smoke but even more so with the aroma of loving deeds done for His glory, i.e., visiting the sick, feeding the hungry, clothing the naked. The offering of incense reminds us of the words of St. Paul, "We are to God the aroma of Christ among those who are being saved and among those who are perishing. To the one we are the smell of death; to the other the fragrance of life" (2 Cor. 2:15-16). If we are "the aroma of Christ to God," what aroma do we spread among those we meet? Does our presence add something to the lives of people or does it detract? Is God's name glorified through our presence or is it defamed? Only a good tree can bear good fruits — fruits that bear a sweet fragrance. Unless we allow Christ to make us new persons, "a new creation," there is no way we can spread the aroma of Christ to others. For the source of that fragrant aroma is the presence of God within.

As we pray in the Supplicatory Canon to Our Lord Jesus Christ: "Jesus, sweet-scented Flower, make me fragrant."

The Perfume Shop

Among the stories of the desert fathers there is this one. "Whosoever enters a perfume shop, even if he does not purchase any perfume, leaves filled with fragrance. The same thing happens to one who associates with holy people. He takes on the spiritual aroma of their virtue." The real perfume shop is the presence of God. Enter there daily through prayer and you will indeed become "the aroma of Christ to God." Each morning spend time with God in prayer, and all day long your life will radiate the fragrance of Jesus.

The Fragrance of Holy Chrism

It is significant that the chrism with which we are anointed in the Orthodox Church following baptism is composed of a mixture of oil and balm with aromatic herbs. In other words, the oil is perfumed. As the newly baptized is anointed, allusion is made to Christ Who came to spread the perfume of the Gospel to all nations, that He "now grant that this perfumed oil . . . may dwell in him (the newly baptized) strongly and continually" (Const. Apost. VII, 44,2).

St. Cyril of Jerusalem wrote: "You were anointed on the nostrils so that, perceiving the perfume (myron) of Christ, you can say, 'We are the sweet perfume of Christ'" (XXXIII, 1092 B).

The Fragrant Clay

An old Persian fable gives us a beautiful picture of the Christian life. One day a traveler sought a place to rest from the hot, burning desert sand. Gradually he became aware of a secret fragrance. Searching, his hand touched a small piece of clay and to his great surprise he found the answer.

"You are just a lump of clay," he marveled. "Tell me," he asked, "where did you get that rare perfume? It has the fragrance of a rose."

"You are right," the clay replied. "I am only a piece of common clay. There is nothing lovely about me. But, Sir, I have been dwelling with a rose."

This is the Christian's beauty secret: dwelling with Jesus Christ, the Rose of Sharon (Song of Solomon 2:1). No one can be unattractive or dull who dwells in God's presence because the very life of God is kindled within him. And everyone can sense it! To return again to the words of St. Paul:

"Wherever we go (Christ) uses us to tell others about the Lord and to spread the Gospel like a sweet perfume. As far as God is concerned there is a sweet, wholesome fragrance in our lives. It is the fragrance of Christ within us, an aroma to both the saved and the unsaved all around us" (2 Corinthians 2:14,15).

St. Gregory of Nyssa wrote about those who in Christ became rivers of perfume:

"The great Paul was such a river of perfumes flowing from the garden of the Church through the Spirit, whose streamlet was Christ's fragrance; and other such rivers were John and Luke, Matthew and Mark, and all the others, the noble plants in the garden of the bride, who were moved by that luminous southern wind to become sources of perfume, shedding forth the fragrance of the Gospels." [12]

On a hospital visit once, I asked to see a certain patient. The nurse replied, "Oh, he's gone, but he left his roses." In the light of Paul's words "Thanks be to God who . . . through us spreads the fragrance of the knowledge of Him everywhere" (2 Cor. 2:14), there is a sense in which it is the business of all of us to "leave our roses." Christ in us is to become a sweet fragrance to those about us.

A Look at the Censer Itself

Let us take a moment to consider the meaning of the censer. It has a basin wherein burns a charcoal on top of which is placed the incense which emits fragrant smoke representing our prayers as they rise to God. Germanos of Constantinople in his work "Mystical Theoria" (Migne 98, 400) interprets the censer itself as representing the human nature of Jesus, the burning coal the divine nature of Jesus, and the smoke the fragrance of the Holy Spirit. One writer interprets St. Germanos as holding the view that the basin of the censer represents the sacred Womb of the Theotokos which bears the divine coal who is Christ, Who in turn fills the universe with fragrance.[13] The Twelve bells on the censer represent the twelve apostles proclaiming the joy of the Gospel to the ends of the earth — the three chains holding the basin represent the Trinity.

The priest offers the following prayer for the blessing of the incense:

We offer incense unto Thee, O Christ our God, for a sweet smelling savour of spiritual fragrance, which do Thou accept upon Thy most heavenly altar; and send down upon us the grace of Thy most Holy Spirit.

The Censing of the Sanctuary

St. Symeon of Salonika explains the censing of the sanctuary by the priest as follows:

"When . . . the priest has given the blessing, he censes the sanctuary, the nave and all present, since all things are sanctified—the things he censes, as being holy; the people present to sanctify them. Thus, beginning at the Holy of holies, the sanctuary, he censes everything in order. However, he does not cense them simply by chance, but he seals and sanctifies and offers the sanctification to Christ, so that it may become acceptable in heaven, and that the grace of the all-holy Spirit may be sent upon us. For this reason let nobody neglect the censing, since through it he receives the grace of the Holy Spirit."[14]

Thus, for St. Symeon of Salonika, censing was the symbol of the presence of the Holy Spirit. We "offer incense" that He may "send down upon us" the grace of the Holy Spirit.

Fr. Robert Taft believes that "the vesperal offering of incense (that) accompanies Psalm 140 . . . has a penitential meaning: it is a symbol of our self-offering of repentance rising with our prayers and our uplifted hands. . . . The theme of repentance for the sins of the day focuses on this evening psalm, the core of vespers which Chrysostom interprets as an efficacious act of perfect contrition. In time this penitential prayer came to be ritualized by the addition of a rite of incense."[15]

We Use Incense at Home

We emphasize the importance of every Orthodox home having a small portable censer next to the family icon. Parents should light the censer regularly, explaining its meaning to the children. A good practice would be for the parent to bless each child in his/her own room with the censer, allowing the fragrant smoke representing the glory of God's presence to fill each room. Imagine how many beautiful memories this act can instill in children. Every time they come to worship as adults later in life, they will be associating the fragrant incense with a host of endearing memories from their family prayers as children at home. Every time they see the priest censing the altar and the people in the liturgy, they will stand in awe in the presence of the Lord. They will see in the rising smoke, their own prayers ascending to God. God is so real, so immanent in Orthodox worship that He can be *seen* in the icon, *heard* in the Gospel reading, *tasted* in the Eucharist, *touched* as we kiss the icon and exchange the kiss of peace, and *smelled* in the fragrance of incense. He can be experienced as a living God through all five senses.

"A Fragrant Offering"

As a rose that is crushed produces a powerful fragrance, even more so, the Body of Jesus when broken on the Cross for our salvation, produced the sweetest fragrance this world has ever experienced. St. Paul alludes to this in Ephesians 5:2 when he writes, "Christ loved us and gave Himself for us, a fragrant offering and sacrifice to God." This idea of a "fragrant offering" has been incorporated into the liturgy itself, specifically in the petitions: "For the precious gifts here offered . . . let us pray . . . that our God who loveth mankind, Who has received them into His holy and heavenly altar for a sweetsmelling savour of spiritual fragrance may send down upon us divine grace and the gift of the Holy Spirit."

May the fragrance of incense that greets us as we enter church ever remind us of Jesus Who "loved us and gave Himself up for us, a fragrant offering and sacrifice to God" (Eph. 5:2).

PRAYER

*In the evening, morning and noontime,
We praise You, we bless You, we give thanks
to You, and we pray to You, O Master of all,
O Lord Who loves humankind. Guide our
prayers aright as an offering of sweet incense
before You; let not our hearts incline
in words or thoughts of wickedness,
but save us from all dangers and from the evil
powers that pursue our souls. For to You,
O Lord, are our eyes directed, and in You
have we hoped. Let us not be put to shame.
For to You belong all glory, honor,
and worship, to the Father and the Son
and the Holy Spirit, now and forever. Amen.*

*Prayer of the Entrance
of the Great Vesper Service*

Chapter 3

Candles: The Inner and The Outer Flame

Someone once called the Orthodox Church "The Candlelight Kingdom." We have candles at Easter, candles at Epiphany, candles at weddings, candles at baptisms, candles on the altar table, candles when we enter church, candles before icons, candles everywhere. They are so much a part of our worship services, that, visiting a country church in Greece, one person said, "Here where to light a candle is to pray."

Why do we use candles? If "to light a candle is to pray," what has prayer to do with lighting candles? Why are they so much a part of Orthodox worship? If to light a candle is a worshipful act, then do I know what is worshipful about it? What, if anything, do candles have to do with God and my faith in Him?

God As Fire and Light

To understand the use and meaning of candles in our worship, we must look to the Bible where God is so often described in terms of fire and light.

We read in Hebrews 12:24, "For our God is a consuming fire."

When God spoke to Moses in the wilderness, He appeared to him as fire in the burning bush. "And the angel of the Lord appeared to him in a flame of fire out of the midst of a bush; and he looked, and lo, the bush was burning, yet it was not consumed" (Exodus 3:2).

When God guided His people to the Promised Land, He used a cloud by day and a pillar of fire by night. We read in Exodus 13:21-22, "And the Lord went before them by day in a pillar of cloud to lead them along the way, and by night in the pillar of fire to give them light . . . the pillar of cloud by day and the pillar of fire by night did not depart from before the people."

When God appeared to Moses on Mt. Sinai, He appeared again as fire. We read in Exodus 19:18, "And Mt. Sinai was wrapped in smoke, because the Lord descended upon it in fire; and the smoke of it went up like the smoke of a kiln, and the whole mountain quaked greatly."

Speaking of the coming of the Messiah, the Prophet Isaiah speaks of Him in terms of light. "The people who walked in darkness have seen a great light; those who dwelt in a land of deep darkness, on them has light shined" (Is. 9:1-2).

Jesus speaks of His presence as fire in Luke 12:49 when He says, "I came to cast fire upon the earth; and would that it were already kindled!"

When the Holy Spirit came to the apostles on the day of Pentecost, He descended upon them in "tongues of fire" (Acts 2:1-4).

Throughout the Gospel of John, Jesus is portrayed in terms of light:

> *Jesus is "The light that shines in the darkness and the darkness has not overcome it" (John 1:5).*
>
> *Jesus said, "I am the light of the world; he who follows me will not walk in darkness, but will have the light of life" (John 8:12).*
>
> *Jesus said to them, "The light is with you for a little longer. Walk while you have the light, lest the darkness overtake you; he who walks in the darkness does not know where he goes. While you have the light, believe in the light, that you may become sons of light."*

When Jesus was transfigured, His countenance shown brighter than the sun.

It is said of St. Sergius of Radonezh that while he was celebrating the divine liturgy, one of his disciples, Simon, beheld a wonderful vision. While the saint was singing the liturgy, Simon saw a flame hovering over the holy table. As St. Sergius was about to receive the Eucharist, the divine fire coiled itself together and entered the sacred chalice. The presence of God appeared as fire.

Candles, Candles Everywhere

Every time we light a candle, then, the flame and the light should remind us of God Who in the history of salvation has appeared time and again as fire and light. Let us look briefly at the meaning of candles as used in our worship. The Sanctuary Lamp, otherwise known as the Ever-Burning Light (Akoimitos) that burns constantly, usually suspended from the ceiling over the Tabernacle on the Holy Table, reminds us of God's constant presence in our midst. He never leaves us or forsakes us. Other candles are extinguished after services but never the Ever-Burning Light. A symbol of God's unfailing presence in our midst, the flame flickers endlessly. Romano Guardini, meditating on the Eternal Light, said, "Lord, that Ever-Burning Light is like my soul which is at all times in Your Presence."

Many Orthodox Christians light a candle upon entering church. This simple act is deeply meaningful. It means that in the liturgy when the word of God is preached, the Holy Spirit will come to remove the veil (2 Cor. 3:15 and 4:6) of blindness from our eyes, the veil of lack of understanding and make the light of Christ shine in our hearts. Lighting a candle on entering church expresses our belief that Jesus is the Light of the World and that, as His disciple, I am called daily to reflect His light in my life. It reminds us that when we were baptized we received Jesus Who is the Light of the World. Like Him, instead of cursing the darkness, we are to be lighting candles of hope and love in the lives of people. As we light that candle in the narthex before we enter church we can pray the beautiful words of the Psalmist, "The Lord is my light and my salvation; whom shall I fear? The Lord is the stronghold of my life; of whom shall I be afraid?" (Psalm 27:1).

We light the Paschal Candle at the midnight Easter liturgy to remind us that Christ has gone on before us into the darkness of death and has overcome that darkness, transforming it into unwaning light. "Come, receive light from the unwaning light and glorify Christ Who is risen from the dead." The Paschal Candle proclaims our faith that the Resurrected Christ "has delivered us from the dominion of darkness and transferred us to the kingdom of His beloved Son, in Whom we have redemption, the forgiveness of sins" (Col. 1:13-14).

When the priest comes out in procession with the Gospel Book during the liturgy, he is preceded by acolytes carrying candles to show that the word of God, to use words of the Psalmist, is "a lamp unto our feet and a light unto our path." The candles that precede the procession with the Gospel Book speak loud and clear. They tell us that the word of God is light for the darkness in which we walk. Its purpose is to prevent us from stumbling; to show us the way; to lead us home to God.

In some Orthodox churches in the Middle East, I have seen an object resembling an ostrich egg suspended immediately above the flickering flame of hanging votive lights. The symbolism of the ostrich egg has to do with the heat produced by the flame of the votive candle. Just as an ostrich must sit on the egg for a long time in order to slowly hatch it with the heat of its body, so the Christian must remain close to the flame of Christ. He must stay close to the church and must nurture his faith through daily prayer and regular communion with Christ through the Eucharist. Only then will faith grow, develop, mature and come to life. The ostrich egg represents the embryonic state of faith which can spring to life through patient and faithful ascesis, producing a life full of the fruits of the Spirit, a life that will glorify the Trinity.

────── *The Candle At the Presanctified Liturgy* ──────

A special rite involving a candle has been incorporated into the Presanctified Liturgy. This rite dates back to the time when it was the purpose of Lent to prepare the catechumens for baptism. While the lesson from Genesis is read, a lighted candle is placed on top of the Gospel book on the holy table. After the lesson, the priest takes the candle and the censer and blesses the congregation with them as he proclaims, "The light of Christ illumines all."

The candle, of course, symbolizes Christ Who is the Light of the World. The fact that it is placed on the Gospel book signifies (1) that Christ is the Light of the World; (2) He is the One Who opened the hearts and minds of His disciples that they might understand the Scriptures; and (3) that all the Old Testament prophecies are fulfilled in Christ, the long-awaited Messiah.

Like the five wise maidens holding their burning lamps, the bride and groom hold candles in the Sacrament of Matrimony to signify their eagerness to receive the Bridegroom Christ when He comes to bless them through the sacrament.

St. Symeon of Thessalonika, the New Theologian, says that the reason vigil lights are placed before the icons of the saints is to show that without the Light, Who is Christ, the saints are nothing. It is only as the light of Christ shines upon them that they become alive and resplendent.

The Feast of Lights

In the early Church, Epiphany—the day of Christ's baptism—became one of the days on which the pagan converts to Christianity were received into the Church through baptism. Each

newly-baptized convert held the baptismal candle during the liturgy. In addition to this, Christians who had already been baptized brought their baptismal candles to church on this day to renew their baptismal vows; to renew the commitment to Christ which they had made at baptism. As a result, everyone in the congregation held a lighted candle on the feast of Epiphany. The churches became a sea of lights. Hence, this day came to be called in Greek "ta Fota" or the Feast of Lights.

The Baptismal Candle

In the early Church the baptismal candle was a symbol that the one baptized had received Christ Who is the Light of the World. In fact, when given the candle at baptism, the newly baptized was also given the injunction of Jesus, "Let your light so shine before men, that they may see your good works and give glory to your Father in heaven" (Matt. 5:16). Kept by the one baptized, the candle was brought to church on feast days, on the anniversary of one's baptism and for the midnight Easter liturgy. If the person married, the same candle was used at the wedding. If ordained, he would light it at his ordination. When the final hour of life approached, it was lit again as the soul went forth to meet its Judge. The baptismal candle was a constant reminder for the Christian to live and die by the light of Christ.

The baptismal candle may be compared to the lamps used in the story of the maidens who awaited the arrival of Christ the Bridegroom in the darkness of the night. When the neophyte was given the lighted candle, he was urged to keep it to meet Christ at His return like the wise maidens who kept their lamps burning for the coming of the Bridegroom. Thus the candle became a symbol of the perseverance of the baptized soul until Christ's return. Among the ancient Greeks the runner who had won the race was not the man who crossed the line in the shortest time, but the man who crossed it in the least time *with his candle still burning.* Our goal as Christians is that we may cross the line into eternity one day with the light of our baptismal faith still shining brightly.

In fact, in the early Church when presenting the candles to the newly baptized, there existed a tradition of admonishing the neophyte with these words, "Receive this candle and keep it burning constantly so that when the Lord comes in the marriage feast of the virgins you may be able to be ushered with the five wise maidens and all the saints into the heavenly courts of life everlasting."

Fr. John of Kronstadt

Fr. John of Kronstadt has written these inspiring words concerning the use and meaning of candles in Orthodox worship:

> *The candles and lamps burning in church remind us of spiritual light and fire, as of the Lord's words:* I am come a Light into the world, that whosoever believeth on me should not abide in darkness; *and again:* I am come to send fire on the earth; and what will I, if it be already kindled? *and again:* Let your loins be girded about, and your lights burning; and ye yourselves like unto men that wait for the Lord, when he will return from the wedding; that when he cometh

and knocketh, they may open unto him immediately; *and* Let your light so shine before men, that they may see your good works, and glorify your Father, which is in heaven.

Do not grudge burning a wax taper before the image of the Lord during prayer; remember that you burn it before Light inacessible, before him who enlightens you with his light. Your candle is as though a burnt offering to the Lord. Let it be a gift to God from your whole heart. Let it remind you that you yourself should also be a burning and shining light. He was, *says our Lord of John the Forerunner,* a burning and a shining light.

I offer light to the Lord, in order that he may bestow the light of grace, the spiritual light, upon me, that he may lead me from the darkness of sin into the light of the knowledge of God and of virtue; I offer fire that the fire of the grace of the Holy Ghost may be kindled in my heart, and that it may quench the fire of the vices of that miserable heart. I bring a light that I myself may become a light, burning and shining to all that are in the church.

It is well to place candles before the images. But it is still better if you bring as a sacrifice to God the fire of your love for him and your neighbor. It is well that the one should accompany the other. But if you place candles before the images, and have no love for God and your neighbor in your heart, if you are grasping, if you do not live in peace with others—then, your offering to God is useless.[16]

Let Your Gift Be the Flame

Maeterlinck recounts an old story that has much food for thought for us today. The story concerns a keeper of the lighthouse on a dangerous and isolated coast. The supply ship was long overdue, and the little community clustered about the lighthouse was in dire straights. Because he loved his neighbors, the lighthouse keeper began sharing with them his surplus stock of oil until finally the oil was exhausted, and one night the beacon on top of the lighthouse failed to burn. That very night, the belated supply ship, in attempting to make its way into the harbor, went on the rocks, and ship, crew, and supplies were lost.

In concluding the story, Maeterlinck says, "See that you give not away the oil of your lamp . . . let your gift be the flame."

"Let your gift be the flame," This is exactly what Jesus tells us: "You are the light of the world. . . . Let your light so shine before men that they may see your good works and give glory to your Father who is in heaven" (Matt. 5:14, 16). As God chose His people of old—the Israelites—to be "a light to the Gentiles," so He has chosen us to be lights to the unbelieving world. Like John the Baptist we are to be burning and shining lights for Jesus. But the question is: How? How can I shine for Jesus? St. Augustine gave the answer centuries ago when he said, "One loving spirit sets another on fire." By our faith, love and hope we are called to light candles of faith, love and hope in others. How easy it is to curse the darkness, but how far better it is to light a candle. If we walk in His light, we will be lighting candles all along the way, bringing not only light but also help and healing to those whose lives we touch.

The Inner Fire

St. John Climacus urges that the life of a repentant person be constantly aflame. The wise and sincere monk is the one who does not allow his inner fire to be extinguished, and who right up to the day he leaves (this life) constantly kindles flame upon flame, ardor upon ardor, longing upon longing, and zeal upon zeal.

This fire is the fire of God's love, poured out in Christ and shed abroad in our hearts by the Holy Spirit. This flame of love kindles an answering fire of faith and love in the believer. It was this flame that burned in the hearts of the two disciples on the road to Emmaus when they said to each other: "Did not our hearts burn within us while He talked to us by the way . . . ?"

For example, here is a devout Christian woman who spends two days a week serving as a volunteer in a large city hospital. A recovered cancer patient, she spends much of her time radiating hope and cheer to others who are going through the same ordeal. So effective is her ministry that doctors, after visiting a depressed cancer patient, will write on the bedside chart, "Have Mrs. X spend time with this person." Why? Why Mrs X? Because doctors know that she has an inner light, that her very presence "lights up candles" of faith and hope in people.

The candles we light in church are not to be left in church but are to be carried out into the world. We come to church to "connect," to establish contact with Jesus Who is Fire and Light. As we commune with Him at the Lord's table and receive His word, we bring ourselves to where He kindles and lights the candle of our spirit. As we pray before the Gospel is read in the liturgy, "O Lord and lover of mankind: make the imperishable light of Thy divine knowledge to shine in our hearts . . ." Just as we carry the light of the Paschal Candle to our homes following the midnight Easter liturgy, so, every Sunday, we can leave the liturgy as living candles that have been lit by the Holy Spirit, pushing forth in different directions, scattering the darkness before us as we press on. We have not only "seen the true light," but the Holy Spirit has also kindled the flame of God's love in our hearts. We leave as burning and shining lights.

Once baptized, we become involved in the life style of the kingdom. We are the reflected lights of the great Light, which is Christ. Frightening as it may seem, the world will know Him because it knows us. There are no secret citizens in the kingdom. Either we will let the light of Christ shine through us by what we are, do, and say—or we will by our defections, block out the light.

Two Candles

On a certain altar table there were two candles. One was burning, the other had gone out. It was sad to look at the dark candle. The burning candle was consuming itself, but it gave light and warmth in the process. Darkness was dispelled, and hearts were kindled by looking at the living flame. The other candle that was unlit remained intact, but it failed in its purpose. Looking at those two candles, a person prayed, "Lord, let me not be like this quenched candle. Let me burn away my life in Thy service."

A mother and her small daughter walked past the house in Springfield, Illinois, where Abraham Lincoln once lived. Seeing the lights burning inside, the little girl said, "Look, Mom. When Mr. Lincoln went away he left the lights on." If we allow Jesus to light the candle which is our life, the light will shine and the influence of our life will continue long after we die. And it will be said of us, too, that when we left this world we "left the lights on."

The Soul is A Lamp

St. Symeon the New Theologian declares that God is fire. The Holy Spirit descended on the Apostles at Pentecost in the form of flaming tongues of fire. He compares the soul to a lamp. Just as a lamp must be adorned with a good supply of oil and trimmed wicks in order to produce fire and light, so the soul must be adorned with all virtues, but beyond that it must receive the fire which is the Holy Spirit. God is fire, he says, and through the Holy Spirit searches for material to set on fire with divine love. We are that material. Jesus came to cast fire not on earth but in our hearts and minds. He came to ignite and illumine the lamp of each person's soul.

We read in Proverbs 20:27, "The spirit of man is the candle of the Lord." The human spirit remains unfulfilled until it is touched by the divine flame.

All candles have one thing in common: they must be lit in order to be useful. If not, they may as well be pieces of pottery.

God created us in many different sizes, shapes and colors. Each of us has a special talent. But, like candles, we are just a decoration in the world unless we are lit to shine for Him.

The Holy Spirit is the Illuminator

God is the One Who lights us with His Holy Spirit. With that Spirit we glow, we give warmth, we make people happy. Have you ever noticed how a true Christian radiates joy? We often say of a real Christian that he lights up the room when he or she walks in.

In fact, there is a story in "The Sayings of the Desert Fathers" about Abba Lot. We read: "Abba Lot went to Abba Joseph and said to him, 'Abba, as far as I can, I say my little office, I pray and meditate, I live in peace and, as far as I can, I purify my thoughts. What else can I do? Then the old man stood up and stretched out his hands towards heaven. His fingers became like ten lamps of oil and he said to him, 'If you will, you can become all flame.'"

The Wax, the Wick and the Flame

"The spirit of man is the candle of the Lord." We can use a votive light to illustrate this. We have three ingredients in the votive light: the wax or oil, the wick and the flame. The wax or oil that feeds the wick and keeps it burning consists of our prayers, our contact with the Lord through the Sacraments, the Bible and the Liturgy. The wick is the spirit of man or the soul. The flame or fire is the Holy Spirit Who lights the wick of our spirit and keeps it aflame for Christ.

As we look through the Scriptures we see how often the Holy Spirit has lit the wick of man's spirit. For example, when Mary said "Yes" to the angel, the wick in her became a flame. When Paul saw and heard Christ on the road to Damascus, the wick in him became a flame. When Joseph obeyed the voice of the angel and took Mary to protect her, the wick in him became a flame. The wick in us can be lit or unlit, inert or alive, depending on whether we ask the Holy Spirit to set us aflame, and depending on whether through prayer and faith we provide the oil that keeps the wick burning. Anastasius of Sinai declared that the wick of the soul that burns now will lead to our ultimate transfiguration with Christ. He has the transfigured Lord say, "It is thus that the just shall shine at the resurrection; thus that they shall be glorified; into my condition they shall be transfigured, in this glory they shall be transfigured, to this form, to this image, to this imprint, to this light and to this beatitude they shall be configured, and they shall reign with me, the Son of God." St. Paul writes that in the resurrection of the dead Jesus will change our lowly body to be like His glorious body" (Phil. 3:21). At that time "The Lord God will be shining on them" (Rev. 22:5) and "We shall be like Him because we shall see Him as He really is" (I John 3:27). Daniel describes those in heaven as follows: "The learned will shine as brightly as the vault of heaven and those who have instructed many in virtue, as bright as stars for all eternity" (Dn. 12:13). What is now only an inner flame will at the resurrection become an outer flame resplendent with God's glory.

Light From Within

It was said of a devout Christian on his death bed: "There was a brightness on his face as he closed his eyes for the last time on earth." When Moses returned from Mount Sinai with the tablets of the law in his hands, his countenance shone brightly. So much so, that the people had to shade their eyes before they could look at him. Where does this outer glow come from, if not from the inner flame of God's presence? There is a little votive light that burns in the soul of each true Christian. If this inner light is kept burning, it will produce a joyful glow on the countenance. Most people are like stained glass windows. They sparkle and shine when the sun is out, but when the darkness sets in, their true beauty is revealed only if there is a light shining from within.

St. Nicephorus wrote concerning the candle that should burn in the soul of every true Christian:

"You, who desire to capture the wondrous divine illumination of our Savior Jesus Christ—who seek to feel the divine fire in your heart—who strive to sense and experience the feeling of reconciliation with God—who, in order to unearth the treasure buried in the field of your heart and to gain possession of it, have renounced everything worldly—who desire the candles of your souls to burn brightly even now, and who for this purpose have renounced all the world—who wish by conscious experience to know and to receive the kingdom of heaven existing within you—come and I will impart to you the science of eternal heavenly life -."

Implanted at Baptism

This inner light is given to us in baptism. As Fr. George Maloney writes:

"This same transfigured Christ is implanted within us in our baptism as an embryonic life. His glorious light is to blaze forth as we yield to His risen, glorious presence within us. Jesus cannot be more transfigured and glorious than He is in our baptism. But it is we, like the apostles, who do not quite see Him in all His transfiguring light at all times. . . . As we die to the darkness of selfcenteredness in our life,

the light of Christ is not only seen by us, but we begin to experience His transfiguring of us into His same glorious light. . . . By His Spirit living within us, Jesus lives in His risen glory within us. Like a leaven, He permeates from within our every part: body, mind and spirit. Each moment is given to us so that we may surrender ourselves to His inner light and be transformed also through a sharing even now of His glorious resurrection." [17]

Phosphoroi: Bearers of Light

For the great saints of the Church there was a real vision of the Light of Tabor. It occurred at various times depending on one's compunction for sin and humility. These saints knew that Jesus, the Light of the World, was shining day and night in their minds and hearts. He was transforming them into a radiant light. They became *phosphoroi,* bearers of the true light. The experience of seeing Jesus as light was so powerful to St. Symeon the New Theologian that he did not know whether he was "in the body or out of the body" (II Cor. 12:2). It was said of Fr. John of Kronstadt: "All is written on Fr. John's face. He is glowing, shining." The inner light produces an outer glow. Did not St. Paul say, "Be aglow with the Spirit"? (Rom. 12:11). When the Holy Spirit is present within, how can there not be an outer glow? When Jesus—the light of the World—is shining in the soul, how can there not be an outer radiance? We read in "The Sayings of the Desert Fathers": "They said of Abba Pambo that he was like Moses, who received the image of the glory of Adam when his face shown. His face shown like lightning, and he was like a king sitting on his throne." [18]

Protect the Flame

Does the flame of God's presence still burn in your soul? The same inner flame the disciples experienced during their walk with Jesus on the Road to Emmaus when they said, "Did not our hearts burn within us when He walked with us?" We read in that great classic of Orthodox spirituality "The Art of Prayer":

"But God gave us a bright lamp when He kindled the grace of the Holy Spirit in our souls. But of those

> *who have received this light, some have made it brighter and clearer, such as Paul, Peter, and all the saints; but others have quenched it, such as the five foolish virgins or those who suffered shipwreck in the faith. . . . And so Paul says, 'Quench not the Spirit.' . . . What quenches it is an impure life. . . . The flame also goes out when there is not enough oil. . . . The Spirit came to you by God's mercy; and so if it does not find corresponding fruits of mercy in you, it will flee from you. For the Spirit does not make its dwelling in the unmerciful soul. . . . Cast aside everything that might extinguish this small flame which is beginning to burn within you, and surround yourself with everything which can feed and fan it into a strong fire (i.e.) . . . solitude, prayer, meditation."* [19]

Protect the flame. Quench it not. Keep the wick burning through ascesis, i.e., repentance, humility, acts of mercy, fasting, solitude and prayer. Our great task is to care for the inner fire not just in order to warm ourselves, but even more so in order to offer warmth and light to lost travellers. Otherwise we are like the Dutch patriot, Vincent Van Gogh, who wrote to his brother, "Dear Theo: There may be a great fire in our soul, yet no one ever seems to warm himself at it and the passers by only see whiffs of smoke coming through the chimney and go along their way."

St. Seraphim of Sarov wrote, "When both the intellect and the heart are united in prayer, and when the thoughts of the soul are not scattered, the heart is warmed by a spiritual heat, the Light of Christ enlightens it and fills the interior man with peace and joy." This does not mean that it will be all radiance and light when we walk with Christ. The inner darkness will still be there. We shall have to struggle against it. But it shall never prevail. "The light shines in the darkness, and the darkness has not overcome it" (John 1:5). We may not shine brightly, and sometimes our lives will be only a glimmer of what they ought to be. But even so, they will be of the light and not of the darkness.

Simone Weil writes in her autobiography of being warmed by the inner flame of a devout Christian she met:

> *There was a young English Catholic . . . from whom I gained my first idea of the supernatural power*

*of the sacraments because of the truly angelic
radiance with which he seemed to be clothed after
going to communion."*

I Am the Lighthouse

A newly commissioned navy captain took great pride in his first assignment to be in command of a battleship. One stormy night the captain saw a light moving steadily in their direction. He ordered the signalman to send the following message.

"Change your course ten degrees to the south."

The reply came back.

"Change your course ten degrees to the *north*."

The captain was determined not to give way to another vessel, and so he sent a counter message.

"Alter your direction ten degrees. I am the *captain!*"

The answer flashed back promptly.

"Alter your direction. I am a lighthouse!"

There are times when we are like that captain. Self-will sets us on a collision course. We stubbornly insist on our own way until the lighthouse of God's word penetrates and reveals the rocky shore ahead. And, if we're smart, we do what the captain must have done. We obey.

May the candle we use so often in our Orthodox worship serve to remind us of God's word shining as a beacon in the darkness to lead us away from the destructiveness of sin to the haven of God's presence.

The Growth of the Inner Light

A Monk of the Eastern Church in his book "The Year of Grace of the Lord" associates the growth of the inner light with the progress of the liturgical year:

"We have already underlined the importance of the theme of light in the Byzantine liturgical year: this divine light first appears with the birth of Jesus, it grows with Him; on Easter night it triumphs over the darkness; at Pentecost it reaches its full zenith. Pentecost is 'the midday flame.' But this development, which the liturgical year expresses, must correspond to a growth of the inner light in our soul. The riches

and symbolism of the liturgical year are worth nothing if they do not help this 'inner light' to guide our life.'

He continues, speaking now of the three conversions in the stages of growth in the spiritual life of a Christian:

"We have said, too, that in spirtual life three stages can be discerned which are comparable to three conversions. The first conversion is the meeting of the soul with our Lord, when He is followed as a Friend and as a Master. The second conversion is a personal experience of pardon and salvation, of the cross and of the resurrection. The third conversion is the coming of the Holy Spirit into the soul like a flame and with power. It is by this conversion that man is established in a lasting union with God. Christmas or Epiphany, then Easter, and finally Pentecost correspond to these three conversions. Alas! It is probable that we have not yet been transformed into a living flame by the many Pentecosts with which already, year after year, we have been liturgically associated. But at least it is good never to lose sight of what graces, what possibilities each Pentecost brings." [20]

Jesus and the Inner Light

If the candle we light in church is just an outward flame; if it does not give expression to the inner flame of the Holy Spirit that burns in our minds and hearts, then the outward act of lighting a candle becomes an empty symbol devoid of meaning. Jesus once told His disciples that there were twelve hours of daylight, during which they could walk without stumbling; but when this world's light went out, and night fell, they would stumble unless they had an inner light to guide them. Jesus had this inner light which guided Him in the dark moments of His life. Through what He did for us at Christmas, Easter and Pentecost, He came to plant this light in us.

The Inner Light in Byzantine Icons

The concept of the inner light has been incorporated into Byzantine iconography. In icons the light of God resides in the inner person and emerges from within. There are no shadows since shadows are seen only when there is outer light. The Source of this inner light, of course, is the Holy Spirit and it is usually expressed through a glow on the face of the one depicted on the icon, which is usually contemplative as one who is looking within. This is in contrast to religious paintings of the West where the light is shown as coming from an outside source with shadows and an outsized halo.

The candles we light in church, then, should be but an outer expression of the light planted in us by Jesus at baptism. In the words of St. Paul, "For it is the God Who said, 'Let light shine out of darkness, who has shone in our hearts to give the light of the knowledge of the glory of God in the face of Christ'" (II Cor. 4:6).

A Word of Caution

A note of caution here. There are many cults that emphasize the Inner Light. They have good things to say about the inner light and the guidance they receive from it. However, by "inner light" they do not mean what we mean: the presence of the Trinity within us. Inner light to them means their own light that emerges from their own thinking. It has nothing to do with God. It is, in fact, a Godless humanism. As G. K. Chesterton so well said, "That Jones shall worship the god within him turns out ultimately to mean that Jones shall worship Jones."

A Christmas Candle in the Window

There is a beautiful Christmas tradition in some European countries of placing a candle in the windows of homes on Christmas Eve. This is done in honor of the Christ Child. If Mary and Joseph are out that night looking for lodging, the candle in the window is a sign of hospitality and welcome to them. But Mary and Joseph are not with us any more. So, the candles indicate to travellers and strangers that there is room for them in those homes on Christmas Eve. Any who are in need are invited in, fed, and sheltered in the name of Christ.

If the inner flame of God's presence is really burning within us, it will express itself outwardly as a sign of hospitality and welcome to all who are lost, offering them the warmth and the light of Christ. It will be an inviting flame, transforming us into burning and shining lights for Christ.

A Son of Light

Legend tells us that once a zealous young man went to St. Francis of Assisi. He asked the saint to teach him how to preach.

"Gladly," said Francis. "Come with me."

All afternoon the young man followed Francis. They paused beneath a tree, and Francis stooped to restore a fallen bird to its nest. They went on and stopped in a field where Francis bent his back to help the laborers load the hay onto a cart. From there they went to the village square, where Francis lifted a bucket of water from the well for an old woman and carried it home for her.

Each time they stopped, the young man was certain that he would hear a sermon —but no wise words of great truth proceeded from the saint's mouth. Finally they went into the church—but Francis only knelt silently to pray.

At last, they returned to the place from whence they had started. "But when," the young man asked, "are you going to teach me how to preach?"

Francis smiled. "I just did."

Francis was a son of light. His entire life shone as a candle for the Lord. "The spirit of man is the candle of the Lord" (Prov. 20:27).

There is much darkness in the world today. Could it be that the darkness is an indictment of us as Christians? As Thomas Merton wrote, "We are supposed to be the light of the world. We are supposed to be a light to ourselves and to others. That may well be what accounts for the fact that the world is in darkness."

Hold A Candle As You Watch and Wait

During his 1960 presidential campaign, John F. Kennedy often closed his speeches with the story of Colonel Davenport, the Speaker of the Connecticut House of Representatives.

One day in 1789, the sky of Hartford darkened ominously, and some of the representatives, glancing out the windows, feared the end was at hand.

Quelling a clamor for immediate adjournment, Davenport rose and said, "The Day of Judgment is either approaching or it is not. If it is not, there is no cause for adjournment. If it is, I choose to be found doing my duty. Therefore, I wish that candles be brought."

Rather than fearing what is to come, we are to be faithful till Christ returns. Instead of fearing the dark, we are to be lights for Christ as we watch and wait.

Let God light the fire of His Presence in the fireplace of your heart that you may become a living candle for the Lord. In the beautiful words of Vladimir Lossky: "The fire of grace, kindled in the hearts of Christians by the Holy Spirit, makes them shine like tapers before the Son of God."

After the Apostles were baptized "with the Holy Spirit and with fire" on Pentecost, they went about lighting fires in others. They did nothing coldly. They were passionate in their love for Jesus. When they prayed, others were warmed by the fire of their closeness to God. When they spoke of Jesus, others were kindled by their zeal. Fire kindles fire. A Christian is not a Christian until his spirit has been touched by the fire of God's Spirit. Then he becomes truly "a candle of the Lord."

PRAYER

Lord, help us not just to light candles in worship but also to be candles lit by the Holy Spirit, spreading, wherever we go, the warmth of Your love and the light of Your Truth.   Amen.

Chapter 4

The Flowering of the Cross: The Cross and Flowers

Let me begin with two stories that express the theme of what we shall study in this chapter.

When Solzhenitsyn was in prison camp, he was so depressed one day that he wished to commit suicide. Suddenly a man came out of nowhere and sat down next to him. They were not allowed to talk so the man took a stick and made the sign of the cross on the dirt floor. Then he wiped it out so the guard would not see it. It was just what Solzhenitsyn needed at that moment. The cross reminded him of God's personal love for him. He took courage to go on.

The next story is told by Ruel Howe. "After a devastating fire that wiped us out, except for the clothes on our backs, my father and I were returning with supplies through the woods from a distant village and found that my mother had arranged a lunch on a fallen log in the middle of which she set a rusty tin can filled with wild flowers.

"They symbolized her capacity to find resources in the midst of heartbreak. In the midst of sadness and loss, the flowers spoke of joy; in the midst of tragedy, hope. Do you have any wild flowers in a rusty tin can not far from your smoking ruins?"

The Veneration of the Cross

On the Third Sunday of Lent, the Church celebrates the Veneration of the Holy Cross. On this day a tray of flowers is prepared and among the flowers is placed the Cross with three candles. The Cross reminds us of the voluntary and victorious death of Christ "for the life of the world," and the three candles are symbolic of the Holy Trinity. Flowers surround the Cross because, in the words of the hymn, "the Cross is the beauty of the Church." They express the refreshment and comfort of the life-giving Cross.

Following the Divine Liturgy, the tray of flowers is placed on the Holy Table and is censed. The priest then takes up the tray and, preceded by acolytes, carries it in procession through the nave. During the procession, everyone is invited to join in the singing of the hymn "Holy God, Holy Mighty One, Holy and Immortal One, have mercy on us."

After circling the interior of the church, the tray is placed on a table in the middle of the solea, as the priest intones "Wisdom, let us be attentive." Then the hymn of the day "O Lord save thy people" is sung by the priest and congregation. After this, all kneel and sing together "We venerate your cross, O Lord, and we glorify Your Holy Resurrection." The congregation then comes to kiss the cross which remains exposed in the middle of the church during the whole week of the feast.

The meaning of the feast is expressed in this troparion from Matins:

"When, on this day, we look at the precious Cross of Christ, in faith let us adore it, let us rejoice, and embrace it ardently, beseeching our Lord, Who of His own choice gave Himself to be crucified on it, to make us worthy of adoring His most precious Cross so that, free from all defilement, we may attain the day of Resurrection."

The Service of the Veneration of the Holy Cross is somewhat unusual when compared to other church celebrations in that it does not commemorate any historical event. It simply was created by the conscience of the faithful as an important observance during the Great Lent and must be understood within the character of the spiritual struggle of Lent which calls us to self-denial, introspection, meditation, prayer, repentance, fasting, alms giving and confession of sins. At this halfway point of Lent, the Cross is raised up to remind us of our spiritual goal of imitating Christ by taking up our own cross. Its purpose is to help us gain strength to continue the struggle. Knowing well the weakness of human nature, the Church places before us at this midpoint of Lent the Holy Cross as a powerful incentive to persevere in the struggle.

On this day every year the Cross is "flowered," to signify that it is the Cross of Jesus that brings new life, in sublime beauty and fragrance, making every true believer "the aroma of Christ to God among those who are being saved" (II Corinthians 2:15).

An Emblem of Victory

In the midst of devastation, suffering and death as symbolized by the Cross, the Church places flowers to prepare us for the vision of the resurrection. As Bishop Kallistos Ware writes, "The dominant note on this Sunday, as on the two Sundays preceding, is one of joy and triumph. In the Canon at Mattins, the irmoi are the same as at Easter midnight, 'This is the day of Resurrection . . . ,' and the troparia are in part a paraphrase of the Paschal Canon by St. John of Damascus. No separation is made between Christ's death and His Resurrection, but the Cross is regarded as an emblem of victory and Calvary is seen in the light of the Empty Tomb."

The dominant hymn for the third Sunday of Lent: "We venerate Your Cross, O Lord, and we glorify your Holy Resurrection" is derived from the Matins service of Easter Sunday: "Having witnessed the Resurrection of the Cross . . ." This same prayer is part of the regular Sunday Matin service. Thus, the Cross and the Resurrection are kept together in Orthodox worship. We are encouraged to look beyond the Cross to see the glory of the Resurrection and the joy of eternal life.

The meaning of this Sunday is expressed in the synaxarion of the day as follows:

> *"On this Sunday, the third Sunday of Lent, we celebrate the veneration of the honorable and Life-*

Giving Cross, and for this reason: inasmuch as in the forty days of fasting we in a way crucify ourselves . . . and become bitter and despondent and failing, the Life-Giving Cross is presented to us for refreshment and assurance, for remembrance of our Lord's Passion, and for comfort. . . . We are like those following a long and cruel path, who become tired, see a beautiful tree with many leaves, sit in its shadow and rest for a while and then, as if rejuvenated, continue their journey; likewise today, in the time of fasting and difficult journey and effort, the Life-Giving Cross was planted in our midst by the holy fathers to give us rest and refreshment, to make us light and courageous for the remaining task. . . . Or, to give another example: when a king is coming, at first his banner and symbols appear, then he himself comes glad and rejoicing about his victory and filling with joy those under him; likewise, our Lord Jesus Christ, who is about to show us His victory over death, and appear to us in the glory of the Resurrection Day, is sending to us in advance His scepter, the royal symbol—the Life-Giving Cross—and it fills us with joy and makes us ready to meet, inasmuch as it is possible for us, the King himself, and to render glory to His victory. . . . All this in the midst of Lent which is like a bitter source because of its tears, because also of its efforts and despondency . . . but Christ comforts us who are as it were in a desert until He shall lead us up to the spiritual Jerusalem by His Resurrection . . . for the Cross is called the Tree of Life, it is the tree that was planted in Paradise, and for this reason our fathers have planted it in the midst of Holy Lent, remembering both Adam's bliss and how he was deprived of it, remembering also that partaking of this Tree we no longer die but are kept alive . . .''

The Four Gardens

The flowers we use on this day remind us that the human race began in a garden (Eden). Jesus suffered his agony in a garden

(Gethsemane). Gethsemane is still there and even today the flowers grow profusely. He was crucified in a garden and buried in a garden (John 19:41). And according to Rev. 2:7, paradise will be a garden. According to Scripture, then, history began in a garden with flowers and there it will end. Through sin man cut himself off from the garden and the tree (Gen. 3:23), but in the end God will bring him back to his proper home and he will find the tree of life freely offered for his use (Rev. 22:2).

Flowers in the Eastern Church

Flowers are used extensively in the religious services of the Eastern Church. From the most ancient times to this day, it is customary for the Patriarch of Jerusalem to make a procession from the Mount of Olives to the City of Jerusalem, as Jesus did on Palm Sunday, preceded by children carrying branches from olive trees. Moreover, the Epitafion or tomb of Jesus is beautifully decorated with flowers for the Good Friday Service of the Lamentation of our Lord's death. On Holy Saturday morning laurel leaves are scattered throughout the church as the priest makes a procession announcing the Resurrection. Flowers are always kept on the empty tomb of Jesus in the Church of the Holy Resurrection in Jerusalem. Worshippers often place flowers before icons as offerings of love. And, of course, flowers are used on the graves of our departed loved ones to express the beauty and joy that spring from our faith in the resurrection of Jesus.

The Special Plant: Basil

But of all the flowers and plants used in Orthodox worship, there is one that has a very special place. It is the plant called basil behind which lies a legend. According to this legend, St. Helen, the mother of Constantine, traveled to Palestine in search of the cross. She looked for it in every corner of the land, and her search turned up not one cross, but three. St. Helen was unsure. "God," she prayed, "reveal to me which of these crosses is the one on which the Christ King died." St. Helen stood the three crosses side by side. One day she noticed a sprig of basil growing from the center cross. Immediately she knew this cross was the real one . . . for basil comes from the Greek word for king. St. Helen fell on her knees before the cross with the sweet green basil, in adoration of the King Who had died upon its beams. Ever since then basil replaced another plant that was used extensively in the worship services of the Old Testament: hyssop. "Purge me with hyssop and I shall be clean" (Psalm 51:7).

This event of the finding of the Cross by St. Helen is celebrated each year on September 14 on the Orthodox Church calendar.

Paradise Lost and Gained In a Garden

F. B. Meyer has written a beautiful meditation on the cross and flowers. He writes,

> "It was in a garden that Paradise was lost, and in a Garden it was regained! The sweet flowers of spring waved their incense-cups around the Cross, on which their Creator, to whose thought they owed their beauty, was dying for man's redemption. . . . Yes, there were flowers at the foot of the Savior's Cross, and they have blossomed at the foot of every cross since His!
>
> Where there is a cross, there will be a garden. . . . Suffer for others in your Gethsemane-garden, and when you have been crucified after that fashion, then look for a garden in bloom. Set up a Calvary in your own heart! Let the cross there be a splint from the Cross of your Savior! Bring there your self-love, your ambitions, your moods and vagrant, selfish thoughts. Fasten your self-life, vain and proud as it is, to the Cross of Jesus, and let it remain there. Then in the garden of your character will arise a profusion of the rarest and sweetest flowers . . .
>
> > Your hearts' a garden God has sown
> > To give your life the work it needed.
> > Some day He'll come to pluck His flowers,
> > So mind you keep your garden weeded."[21]

The Cross: The Favorite Christian Symbol

The cross is a favorite symbol among Orthodox Christians. It appears on almost everything used in God's service: altars, linens, churches, books, vestments. During the liturgy we make the sign of the cross countless times. In our personal devotions we cross ourselves morning and evening, before and after all our prayers, in temptation, in bodily dangers, before every important action or undertaking.

St. Cyril of Jerusalem wrote in the 4th centrury: "Let us then not be ashamed to confess the Crucified. Be the cross our seal, made with boldness by our fingers on our brow and in everything; over the bread we eat and the cups we drink, in our comings in and in our goings out; before our sleep, when we lie down and when we awake; when we are traveling and when we are at rest."

We Cross Ourselves

I wonder if we have ever pondered how rich in meaning is the sign of the cross as we Orthodox Christians make it?

To make the sign of the cross we join the thumb, the index and the middle finger of the right hand at their tips, and at the same time we rest the fourth and little finger in the palm of the

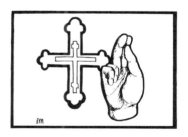

hand. First we touch the forehead, then the breast and immediately following the right and left shoulder in that order. At the end we let the hand fall to the side as we make a bow. The thumb, the index and middle finger touching each other at their tips, represent the Holy Trinity: God the Father Who created us, God the Son Who saved us, and God the Holy Spirit Who abides in us: three persons in one God—the Holy Trinity. Then we let the fourth and little fingers representing the two natures of Jesus— human and divine—drop into the palm of the hand to denote that the Son of God *"came down from heaven"* and became man for our salvation. Thus, we make the sign of the cross to remind ourselves of who God is and what He did for us. Every time we cross ourselves we recall the great price He paid to redeem us.

Our Response to Christ's Sacrifice

But through the sign of the cross we express also *our response* to the sacrifice of Christ: we place our hand to the forehead and promise that with God's help we shall endeavor to know Him with all our mind; we place our hand to our breast promising that our purpose in life will be to *love* God with all our heart; then we place our hand to the right and left shoulders promising to *serve* God with all our soul and strength. Thus we give expression to the great Biblical commandment: "Thou shalt love the Lord thy God with all thy mind, and with all thy heart, and with all the strength, and with all thy soul." Finally we bow to acknowledge that we and all humans are under God's dominion and rule. The sign of the cross, then, as we Orthodox Christians make it expresses some of the most basic and fundamental teachings of our Orthodox faith: the Trinity, the Incarnation, the great Biblical commandment, and commitment to Christ. It is the body praying together with the soul. The *whole person* prays to God.

Fr. John of Kronstadt

Fr. John of Kronstadt wrote: "In making the sign of the cross believe and constantly remember that your sins are nailed to the cross. When you fall into sin, at once judge yourself sincerely, and make the sign of the cross upon yourself, saying, Lord, Thou that nailest our sins to the cross, nail also this my sin to thy cross, and have mercy upon me after thy great goodness, and you will be cleansed from your sin."

Weldon Hardenbrook, speaking on the marking of one's body with the sign of the Cross, writes: "And when temptation comes, or when our bodies want to take control with their passions, physically making a cross on our bodies brings the power of the cross into action—like an arrow released from a bow. Let's face it! We put the cross on our steeples, Bibles, neck chains, tombstones and everything else, and it's time to sign ourselves with it."[22] He was speaking to Protestant Christians who do not customarily make the sign of the cross on their bodies.

St. John Chrysostom On the Cross

St. John Chrysostom offered the following encomium on the Cross of Jesus:

"*The Cross has dissolved hatred towards man, has brought reconciliation, has made the earth heaven, has mingled men with the angels, has conquered the bastion of death, has neutralized the strength of the devil, has dismissed the power of sin, has rid the earth of error, has restored the truth, has driven away the demons, has torn down pagan temples, has upset sacrificial altars, has dispelled the smell of burnt offerings, has planted virtue, has founded churches.*

The Cross is the Will of the Father, the Glory of the Son, and the Joy of the Spirit, the Pride of Paul.

The Cross is brighter than the sun and gayer than its ray.

The Cross has torn our mortgage, has rendered useless the prison of death.

The Cross is the proof of the love of God, the unshaken wall, the unconquered weapon, the security of the rich, the richness of the poor, the weapon of the threatened, the rebuke of the passions, the kingdom of virtue, the wonderful and strange sign.

The Cross has opened paradise, has admitted the thief, and has guided the human race from impending disaster to the kingdom of God."

St. John of Damascus On the Cross

St. John of Damascus praises the Cross with these beautiful words:

"*Every action and every miracle of Christ are most divine and marvellous, but the most marvellous of all is His Honorable Cross. For no other thing has subdued death, expiated the sin of the first parents, destroyed Hades, bestowed the resurrection, granted power to us of condemning death itself, prepared the return to original blessedness, opened the gates of Paradise, given our nature a seat at the right hand of God, and made us the children of God, save the Cross of Our Lord Jesus Christ. The death of Christ on the*

Cross clothed us with the hypostatic Wisdom and Power of God.''

The Power and Wisdom of God

St. Paul says of the Cross:

"For the Jews demand signs and the Greeks seek wisdom, but we preach Christ crucified, to the Jews a scandal, to the Greeks foolishness, but to those who are called, both Jews and Greeks, Christ the Power of God and the Wisdom of God" (I. Cor. 1:24).

The early Fathers tell the story of the devil speaking and saying, "Three things I fear in Christians: that in which they bathe (baptism); that which they eat in church (the Eucharist), and that which they wear around their necks (the Cross)."

It is the life-giving Cross of Christ which repels the devil; which saves us; the Cross we must take upon ourselves if we will be saved; the Cross by which we must enter into and share in the victorious Resurrection of Christ.

In the Saviour's Cross is found all there is of the grace of God:

His forgiveness for my guilt!
His peace for my turmoil!
His cleansing for my impurity!
His power for my weakness!
His courage for my fear!
His love for my bitterness!
His victory for my defeat!

When people who believe in astrology ask me: "Under what sign were you born?" I like to tell them: "Under the sign of the Cross. By this sign I was baptized. By this sign I live. By this sign I conquer. By this sign I shall die." As St. Paul says, "I have been crucified with Christ. It is no longer I who live but Christ who lives in me; and the life I now live in the flesh I live by faith in the Son of God who loved me and gave Himself for me" (Gal. 2:20).

On the cross Jesus broke the power of sin and Satan.
On the cross Jesus paid the penalty we could not pay.
On the cross Jesus gave Himself for us.
On the cross Jesus opened the gates of heaven for us.

*On the cross Jesus won eternal life with God for us.
On the cross Jesus showed that forgiving people in love is the best way to live.
On the cross Jesus saved us.*

Fyodor Dostoyevsky said, "It is the Cross that focuses the human condition in all its bitterness and all its horror, and it is the Resurrection that proclaims the final response of God: His promise of freedom from sin, the overcoming of death, and abundant life at last."

The Great Plus Sign

The Cross of Jesus is in reality a plus sign— the greatest plus sign this world has ever known. It is God's great plus sign for you and me. It means that God offers me great pluses as I go through life:

1. I need not be alone with my problems and troubles. I can have the great *plus* of God's presence, His guidance, direction and wisdom.
2. Sinful man *plus* God's mercy equals forgiveness.
3. Confused man *plus* Christ equals new purpose, new meaning, a totally new person.
4. Guilt-ridden man *plus* Christ equals "the peace of God that passes all understanding."
5. Weak man *plus* Christ equals strength. "I can do all things through Christ who strengthens me" (St. Paul).
6. Despairing man *plus* Christ equals hope. The Cross was not the end for Jesus; neither will it be the end for those who believe in Him The risen Christ will have the last word. And the last word is: "In the world you have tribulation, but be of good cheer, I have overcome the world" (Jesus).

No Cross No Resurrection

It is simply not true, as some have held, that the Eastern Church has emphasized the Resurrection while the Western Church has placed the accent on the Cross of Christ. The two cannot be separated and are never separated in Orthodox doctrine and worship. We preach Christ crucified and resurrected. The Cross is central to Orthodox Christianity: no cross, no resurrection! Orthodox Christianity is not a religion of the Resurrection only; it is also a religion of the Cross. We preach Christ crucified and risen. Both! Not just one! It is from the Cross that joy has come to the world. "We venerate Your Cross, O Lord, and we glorify your holy Resurrection."

The Cross in Orthodox Hymnology

Orthodox hymnology exalts the Cross as ZOEFOROS (life-giving). It is called ZOE KAI ANASTASIS (life and resurrection). It is hailed as a "ladder to heaven": "O divine ladder, by which we climb to heaven" (Matins hymn—Exaltation of Cross, September 14). "O Cross, open the doors of heaven to those who love Thee" (Hymn of Small Vespers of the Saturday before the Third Sunday of Lent).

Consider some of the inspired hymns of the Orthodox Church as they speak of the Cross:

"Thou has given thyself to be crucified for me, in order to convey to me my pardon, Thou hast allowed thyself to be pierced for me, in order to make rivers of living water flow. Thou hast allowed thyself to be nailed, in order that I may believe the depth of thy passion and that I may exclaim: 'Glory to thy Cross, O Christ, giving life, glory to thy passion, O Savior!'" (Holy Thursday).

"Joy to thee, O Cross, which contains life, the gate to paradise, the strength of believers, the protection of the Church, by which corruption has disappeared and the power of death was removed; thee, by which we are raised from earth to heaven, invincible arm against demons, the praise of martyrs, the beauty of the faithful, the haven of salvation, granting the world great mercy" (Great Vespers, September 13).

"Approach and take the water which never dries up and which gushes before you by the gift of the

Cross. Here we can see the holy wood, the source of the gift, impregnated by the blood and water of the Lord of all, who was lifted up voluntarily on the Cross and thereby has lifted up men" (Matins, Third Sunday of Lent).

Church Fathers' Encomium to the Cross

St. Athanasios wrote:

"By the sign of the cross . . . all magic is stayed, all sorcery confounded, all the idols are abandoned and deserted, and all senseless pleasure ceases, as the the eye of faith looks up to heaven from the earth" ("On the Incarnation").

St. Cyril of Jerusalem (A.D. 315-385):

"It (the Cross) is a powerful safeguard . . . a grace from God, a badge of the faithful, and a terror to devils . . ."

St. Ephrem the Syrian (+ 373):

'The Cross is — the resurrection of the dead.
The Cross is — the hope of Christians.
The Cross is — the staff of the lame.
The Cross is — the consolation of the poor
The Cross is — the dethronement of the proud.
The Cross is — the hope of the hopeless.
The Cross is — the helm of those who sail.
The Cross is — the harbor of the storm-tossed.
The Cross is — the father of orphans.
The Cross is — the comfort of the afflicted.
The Cross is — the protector of youth.
The Cross is — the glory of men.
The Cross is — the crown of the aged.
The Cross is — the purity of virgins.
The Cross is — the bread of the hungry and the fountain of the thirsty.

. . . Therefore, let us make the sign of this Life-Giving Cross on our forehead, lips and breast. . . . Let us not leave the Cross even for one hour, even for one moment, and let us not do anything without it, but *whether we are going to sleep, or getting up; whether we are eating or drinking, whether we are traveling on land, sailing the sea, or crossing rivers, we should adorn all the members of our body with the sign of the Life-Giving Cross.''*

Chapter 5

The Ladder to Heaven

On the Fourth Sunday of Lent the Church calls attention to St. John of the Ladder (Climacus) who lived in the seventh century. He is held up before us during the season of Lent as an example of penitence. St. John (580-650 A.D.) was the saintly abbott of the Monastery of St. Catherine of Mt. Sinai. Although his feast falls on March 30, the custom of celebrating it on the Fourth Sunday of Lent came into being because his famous spiritual work, "The Ladder of Divine Ascent," was read — and still is — at table in monasteries around the middle of Lent. From this work he came to be known as St. John Climacus (from the Greek word *klimax:* ladder). This famous work, reminiscent of the ladder in Jacob's dream that extended from heaven to earth, is made up of 30 steps leading toward the spiritual perfection of man. Each step represents one year in the life of Christ to the age of His baptism and offers directions to those who would follow the injunction of Jesus: "Be perfect as your heavenly Father is perfect." The book consists of spiritual exercises through which the Christian can reach the highest point of spiritual perfection and thus become a partaker of divine life receiving the fullness of life in Christ. "The Ladder of Divine Ascent" includes a detailed classification of the passions. The focus of its monastic spirituality is the invocation of the name of Jesus. St. John places monasticism in proper perspective when he writes that it has no value if it is not an expression of love. Thus the hymn says of him at vespers: "Thus it is that Thou dost entreat us: love God so that ye may live in His eternal goodwill, and let nothing be set higher than this love."

The hymns of his feast extol him as "an angel in human body" who by "fasting, vigilance and prayers received heavenly gifts to heal the sick and the souls who come to him in faith." "As thy body became thin through abstinence," we sing, "so didst thou renew the power of thy soul, enriching it with heavenly glory." A hymn from vespers calls him, "the pride of ascetics, an angel on earth, the man of God in heaven, the adornment of the world, the flower of virtue and good deeds. Planted in the house of God, he blossomed with justice like a cedar tree in the wilderness. He helped the flock of Christ to grow in holiness and righteousness and justice."

Jacob's Ladder

Since "The Ladder of Divine Ascent" is based on Jacob's dream of a ladder, let us briefly review that famous dream. Most of us are acquainted with the story of Jacob's dream; how he laid himself down to sleep in the wilderness one night with a stone for a pillow and dreamed of seeing a ladder set up between heaven and earth; how he saw angels ascending and descending on the rungs of the ladder; and how God spoke to him in that dream from the top of the ladder. And how Jacob said when he woke up, "Surely the Lord is in this place and I knew it not."

Jacob had committed a terrible sin. He had betrayed his brother and his father, lied, connived, cheated. He had thus cut himself off from God. He could not on his own build a ladder by which to climb back into his broken communion with God. Yet a ladder there had to be, between God in heaven and this sinful, frail child of dust on earth. God builds the ladder in Jacob's dream and comes down to him. In this dream we see God taking the initiative, making it possible for us to come to Him and for Him to come to us.

The dream was the turning point in Jacob's life. From then on he was God's man. He dedicated himself to the service of the Lord. For he had seen the God who hears and answers prayer; the

God who built a ladder from heaven to earth to speak to him; the God who in speaking to a sinner like Jacob had proven Himself kind and merciful beyond comprehension.

It would be many long years before Jacob's dream would come true; for the coming of Christ was many long ages in the future. But in Jacob's dream of the ladder, God promises to bridge the gap between heaven and earth, between God and man. One day the dream would come true in the flesh.

The Fulfillment of Jacob's Dream

We leave the Old Testament and we come now to the New Testament. We hear Jesus saying in St. John's Gospel 1:51, *"Verily, verily, I say unto you, hereafter ye shall see heaven open, and the angels of God ascending and descending upon the Son of man."* With these words Jesus recalls Jacob's dream of the ladder and tells His disciples that they are about to see the ancient dream fulfilled before their very eyes — in the Son of Man; for Christ Himself is the ladder, linking heaven and earth.

No longer then do we need to dream of a ladder between heaven and earth whereby God might come to us and we might climb to Him. Now in Christ we have Jacob's dream come true. Because Jesus paid the price for our salvation, the great gulf is bridged. Our fellowship with Him is restored. Jesus is Emmanuel, i.e., God with us. He is the Ladder.

Man's sin had severed us from God, but Jesus became the mediator between God and man. He is the way by which the glory of God comes down to us and we ascend to the glory of God.

The ladder that God built from heaven to earth leads directly to your heart and mine. It is here that the Lord Jesus wishes to dwell more than anywhere else. God is present everywhere in the universe but his favorite dwelling place is your heart and mine. "Behold, I stand at the door and knock," says Jesus, "if anyone hears my voice and opens the door I will come in to him . . ." (Rev. 3:20).

A Continuing Ascension

Christ's coming into the world marks the opening of heaven. He came down the ladder from heaven and ever since then heaven has remained open. As the ladder, Jesus is the only way to communion with the Father and the Holy Spirit. There is a constant stream of traffic on that ladder. Those angels ever going up and coming down are our prayers. Up to gain help and inspiration — down to bring a little bit of heaven, a breath of Godly air into this world of struggling humanity. "Prayer," writes St. John of the Ladder, "is a continuous ascension to heaven." We may add, so is the liturgy and the reading of God's word — a continuous ascension to where God is.

Metropolitan Emilianos Timiadis likens the Church unto a ladder: "The Church . . . is the mystical ladder on which man ascends to God and God descends, so that a real ascent and descent (anabasis and katabasis) takes place, resulting in the blessed meeting between Creator and creature."[23]

The Mystic Ladder

F. B. Meyer calls Jesus the "mystic ladder":

"Let us think of that mystic ladder which is Jesus Christ our Lord, by which He descended to our humanity and ascended to the Throne of God. He is the Way by which the sons of ignorance and night can pass upward to the eternal Light and Love. Where are you? It may be . . . in a humble cottage, in the crowded city, lying on a bed of pain in the hospital ward! Wherever you are, Jesus finds you out and comes to just where you are. The one pole of the ladder is the gold of His Deity, the other the silver of His Manhood, which is placed against your life. Transmit to Him your burdens of sin and care and fear. Surely the Lord is in this place, and I knew it not. We have a Mediator between God and man, the Man Christ Jesus. None of us is outside God's loving thought and care. There is always a linking ladder between ourselves and Heaven, and God's angels still pass to and fro, sent forth to minister to the heirs of salvation. Let us see to it that we are at the foot of the ladder to claim our share in the blessings which they bring to earth."[24]

The Ladder Is Still There

Several years ago an interesting cartoon appeared in one of the newspapers on Lincoln's birthday. It represented a log cabin close to the base of a high mountain. On the mountain-top was shown the White House. Against the side of the mountain rested a ladder, its foot touching the cabin at the bottom, its uppermost rung reaching to the White House. The cartoon bore the caption:

"The Ladder Is Still There."

It is a sermon in one sentence.

It was as a ladder that God came to us in Christ. He bridged the distance between God and man. He came down to earth to raise us to heaven. He became human that we might become divine, "partakers of divine nature." He came to elevate us from mere existence to fullness of life. He came to lift us from ignorance of God to such personal familiarity with Him that we could address Him as "Our Father." He came to raise us from weakness to power: ". . . you shall receive power when the Holy Spirit has come upon you" (Acts 1:8). He came as a ladder to raise us from the inner hell of sin and guilt to the heavenly joy of God's forgiveness. He came to raise us from the grave of sin and death to freedom and life.

Jesus came as a ladder to connect us with God. And . . . "The ladder is still there."

Interesting cartoon isn't it? A log cabin at the bottom, the White House at the top with a ladder in between. The "log cabin" represents our poverty, our weakness, our sinfulness, our emptiness, our hell, our death. The "White House" represents all that God craves for us to have: forgiveness, fullness of life, a personal love relationship with Him, free access to His presence, power, peace, joy. Christ is the ladder that leads us from emptiness to fullness, from weakness to power, from death to life.

Not A Ladder of Worthiness

It was not Jacob who built the ladder to God. It was God Who let down the ladder from heaven and came to where sinful Jacob was. It is impossible for us to earn salvation by climbing the ladder to God and meeting Him on the topmost rung of the ladder of worthiness. The only way to get to God is for God to come to us through the incarnation and meet us as sinners on the bottommost rung of the ladder. The Gospel begins not with our erecting a  ladder of reasoned argument or moral achievement and trying to climb from earth to heaven. It begins with God letting down the ladder and coming to where we are, entering our lives, casting out our devils, and destroying our death.

So, God is no longer at the top of the ladder. He is with us at the bottom of the ladder; nay, He is with us on the ladder itself. There are those who look upon Christianity as an impossible ideal. They conceive of Christ as standing on top of a Mt. Everest, calling out to us to struggle and climb to where He is. But Christ does not stand at the top of the ladder of Mt. Everest calling on us to follow Him to the top. He comes down to the bottom of the ladder, to where we are, and climbs the ladder with us, step by step. There is traffic on the ladder — more than just angels ascending and descending. In the words of Fr. Dumitru Staniloae: ". . . not only do we ascend to communion with the Supreme Person, but that Person descends to us, too. For love requires the movement of each one of those who love each other toward the other. God gives Himself to man through everything, and man to God."

The Upward Climb

The Ladder of Divine Ascent shows us that an upward journey begins at baptism. To be baptized marks the first step or rung on the ladder to heaven. We must not remain on the first rung of the ladder to heaven, but proceed to the next and the next. There are those who will object and say that we Orthodox are denying that salvation is a gift of God when we begin talking about climbing a ladder to God. This is obviously false since we do not make or climb our own ladder. The Ladder is a Gift; it is Christ Himself. Let us use an example. If a poor young man is given a scholarship by a rich benefactor, the lad is given something he could never achieve on his own: a very great gift. But the young man has to be prepared to work, study and toil hard as a student if he is to realize the full benefit of what he has been given. This is then why it is necessary for us to climb the ladder that God has given us in Christ. God gives us the ladder as a gift. The ladder is none other than Christ, but once we are baptized and accept Jesus as Lord, the task of climbing the ladder, or following Christ, begins.

There is a story of a religious man who dreamed he was building a ladder to heaven. When he did a good deed, the ladder went up one more step. When he gave a dollar to charity, he added another step. When he joined the church, the ladder went up 10 steps. Higher and higher went the ladder 'til it reached beyond the clouds and out of sight. As the end of his life neared, the man thought that surely the ladder would extend clear up into heaven by then. So, confidently stepping off the top of the ladder, thinking it was heaven, he found nothing there and went tumbling head over heels to his ruin. Awakening from his dream, he remembered the words of Jesus, "He that . . . climbeth up some other way, the same is a thief and a robber" (John 10:1). The ladder is the gift of God's grace. It can never be built by our virtues and good deeds.

Grow By Climbing

The very meaning of ladder associates itself with progress and growth. As Thomas Huxley wrote, "The rung of the ladder was not meant to rest upon, but only to hold a man's foot long enough to enable him to put the other somewhat higher." This is why the ladder is projected as a meaningful symbol of spiritual growth during Lent. Thus, spirituality according to St. John Climacus, is not mere perfectionism ("I have arrived! I have made it!") but a never-ending process of climbing and growth leading to new levels of knowledge of God and holiness. Our walk with God in Christ following baptism is a journey onward and upward toward the goal of theosis, i.e., becoming like Christ. It is steady progress one rung at a time. St. John Climacus himself warns: "You will be rejected if you have the effrontery to leap to the top of the ladder of love."

Professor Panagiotes Chrestou speaks of the never-ending spiritual climb when he writes, "Gregory of Nyssa had earlier indicated that he recognized only one limitation in perfection, that it has no limit. When we climb the ladder of spiritual progress, we will never be able to stop ascending; for there is always a step above the step we occupy and there is no summit. Man continuously becomes more spiritual and his spiritual food continuously increases, without his growth ever ending."[25]

The Four Steps of The Ladder

Theophan the Recluse has written on the four steps of the ladder:

> *"Remember the wise teaching of St. John of the Ladder. He describes the way of our ascension to God in the form of a ladder with four steps. Some people, he says, tame their passions; others sing, that is, pray with their lips; the third practise inner prayer; finally the fourth rise to seeing visions. Those who want to ascend these four steps cannot begin from the top, but must start from the bottom; they must step onto the first rung and so ascend to the second, then to the third, and finally to the fourth. By this ladder everyone can ascend to heaven. First you must work on taming and reducing passions; then practise psalmody — in other words, attain the habit of oral prayer; after this, practise inner prayer; and so at last reach the step from which it is possible to ascend to visions. The first is the work of the novice; the second is the work of those who are progressing; the third, of those who have progressed to the end; and the fourth is reserved for those who have achieved perfection."*

In Orthodox theology salvation is not static but dynamic; it is not a state of being, a state of having arrived, a state of having made it, but a constant movement or climbing toward theosis, toward Christ-likeness, toward receiving the fullness of God's life.

Growth On An Ascending Scale

F. B. Meyer gives substance to the idea of constant progress on the ladder of divine ascent when he writes:

> *"God's dealings with us are on an ascending scale. If we see clearly the lowest rung in the heavenly*

ladder, the veil of mist will depart and we shall see the next above it, and then the next, and, in due order, the next; and so the steps that slope away through darkness up to God will always be beckoning to greater and yet greater things.

Have you known Christ as the Word? He is more; both Spirit and Life. Has He become flesh? You shall behold Him glorified with the glory He had before the world began. Have you known Him as Alpha? He is also Omega.

Have you met John? You shall meet One so much greater, that the latchet of His shoes the Baptist shall deem himself unworthy to unloose. Have you beheld the Lamb on the Cross? You shall behold Him in the midst of the throne. Have you seen the Spirit descend like a dove on one head? You shall see Him come as a fire upon an unnumbered multitude.

Do you acknowledge Him as King of Israel? You shall hear the acclamations that salute Him as King of the world.

Live up to all you know, and you shall know more. Be all you can, and you shall become more. Do all that your two talents permit, and you will find yourself ruler over four cities.'' [26]

―――――――――― *Where Is The Ladder?* ――――――――――

St. Isaac the Syrian answered this question when he wrote:

"Enter eagerly into the treasurehouse (the heart) that lies within you, and so you will see the treasurehouse of heaven. For the two are the same, and there is but one single entry to them both. The ladder that leads to the Kingdom is hidden within you, and is found in your soul. Dive into yourself, *and in your soul you will discover the rungs by which you are to ascend.''* [27]

What Are the Rungs?

In describing the rungs on St. John's Ladder of Divine Ascent, M. Heppell writes: "His thirty progressive steps may perhaps be regarded as falling into two sections. Steps 1-26 are mainly concerned with an analysis of the principal vices which must be mastered if progress is to be made in the spiritual life, and with suggestions as to how they are combated, followed by the virtues of spiritual warfare. Steps 27-30 speak, on the other hand, of solitude, prayer, dispassion (apatheia) and love, the virtues of the victor's positive achievement."[28]

Some of the other rungs on the Ladder of Divine Ascent are: repentance, remembrance of death, mourning which causes joy, meekness, poverty, bodily vigil, humility, holy solitude, prayer: the mother of virtues.

The Jesus Prayer is one such sung. Henri Nouwen writes about it: "Such a simple, easily repeated prayer can slowly empty out our crowded interior life and create the quiet space where we can dwell with God. It can be like a ladder along which we can descend into the heart and ascend to God."[29]

Another important rung of the ladder of divine ascent is inner desire and perseverance. St. Gregory of Nyssa stresses this when he writes, "Having once put your foot on the ladder which God is leaning against, go on climbing . . . every rung leads up to the beyond. . . . Finding God means looking for Him tirelessly. . . . To see God means never to cease to desire Him."

One Rung At a Time

Each rung on the ladder is there to hold your foot just long enough to step higher. It wasn't put there for you to park on it permanently. As someone said, "You have to climb all the steps to get to the top, but you don't have to build a nest on them." The purpose of the ladder is to help you keep climbing upward and onward. The one who succeeds is the one who perseveres; the one who fights just one more round. When we consider that our goal in life is theosis, becoming like God in Christ, the goal on the very top of the ladder of divine ascent may seem formidable, sometimes even impossible. But remember the image of the ladder. It speaks to us. It tells us that the way to the goal is one small rung at a time. It can be fatal to try to leap rungs on a ladder. One sure step at a time makes it to the top, always remembering that Jesus is not waiting for us at the top of the ladder. He is on the ladder itself, helping us each step of the way.

There is an ancient icon of the Heavenly Ladder at the Monastery of St. Catherine at Mt. Sinai. It portrays monks climbing a ladder to heaven. Winged devils interfere to impede the ascent of some monks, dragging them down into the open mouth of hell. They are shown being pulled off the ladder and falling into hell. Christ is shown as standing in heaven at the top of the ladder welcoming St. John Climacus who stands at the topmost rung of the ladder. As effective as the icon is, it does not tell the whole story. Christ does not remain at the top of the ladder. His presence should also be portrayed on the ladder. We are not at the mercy of the devil. Emmanuel — God with us — is on the ladder with us. His strengthening presence enables us to resist the onslaughts of the evil one.

Climbing An Extension Ladder

Climbing an extension ladder is a scary experience. When you begin, the ladder seems wobbly and unsteady. But the higher you climb, the more you begin to discover that the weight of your body combines with gravity to steady the ladder. So, the higher you climb, the safer you feel.

Is it not the same when you first begin to climb the ladder of faith? You feel scary at the beginning, shaky and insecure. But the higher you climb, one day of trust at a time, the more you discover that the weight of your trust in God combines with His love for you to give you a steady and secure feeling.

Steps

Romano Guardini sees the steps used in church buildings as rungs on the ladder of divine ascent. He writes, "So the steps that lead from the street to the church remind us that in going up unto the house of prayer we are coming nearer to God; the steps from the nave to the choir, that we are entering in before the All-Holy.

The steps between the choir and the altar say to whoever ascends them the same words that God spoke to Moses on Mount Horeb: 'Put your shoes off your feet, for the place whereon thou standest is holy ground.' The altar is the threshold of eternity."[30]

Another Ladder

The image of the ladder held up before us by St. John Climacus speaks loudly and clearly to modern man. Every one of us is climbing some kind of a ladder in this age of "upward mobility." People today spend a whole lifetime, sacrificing even family and health, in order to climb a ladder — not the ladder of divine ascent but another ladder — the ladder of worldly success. Yet how often we come to discover in the end that all was in vain because we placed the ladder against the wrong building. The goals for which we sacrificed our all remain unfulfilled. We end up with an inner emptiness and void that is terribly painful and so unbearable that it often leads to suicide.

Richard Armour expressed the futility of climbing this worldly ladder of success when he wrote:

Success, up rung by rung.
Should be in good condition now,
Although no longer young.

It took some pull, not only with
Each strongly muscled arm
But with the facial muscles that
Forced smiles to give them charm.

Now at the upper level and
Inclined to rest a bit,
They should be warned that it is now
That they should most keep fit.

They must eat sparingly, lift weights,
Do pushups and the rest,
To feel (and most of all to look)
Their very, very best.

For they are watched for weakening
Or aging, any trace,
By those, including long-time friends,
Who'd like to take their place.

The only real ladder of success is the one about which Jacob dreamed in the Old Testament and which Jesus actually established through His incarnation, death, resurrection and ascension. It is the ladder that God let down to sinful Jacob in the wilderness to assure him of God's Presence, His love and forgiveness. He comes to us again and again piercing the darkness of sin and death. He descends to us to help us ascend to Him. He descends to the very door of our soul and knocks, seeking entrance.

God first let this ladder down into your soul when you were baptized. It is still there. God will never remove it. So, dive into your soul and start climbing it one step at a time using the rungs of faith, love, hope, prayer, humility, repentance, gentleness, kindness, self-control, joy, peace, obedience. It is truly a ladder of divine ascent for it leads to the God of peace and glory.

Spiritual Gems From St. John Climacus

M. Heppell says that "reading the *Ladder* offers a rich reward. There are many passages of profound insight, often vividly expressed; sometimes these occur unexpectedly in the middle of a series of almost trite remarks, like gleams of spiritual light. Here, in such passages, all who are humble and sincerely desire to 'know themselves' as the first step towards inner harmony and spiritual progress can find help and enlightenment . . ."[31]

Here are some of those spiritual gems:

"It is the property of men to fall and to rise again as often as this may happen. But it is the property of devils and devils alone, not to rise once they have fallen."

"Repentance is the daughter of hope and the denial of despair."

"Prayer is a continuous ascension to heaven."

"Repentance is the renewal of baptism. Repentance is a contract with God for a second life."

"A servant of the Lord is he who in body stands before men, but in mind knocks at heaven with prayer."

Asked about how he prays he said, "I have the habit . . . at the very beginning, of collecting my thoughts, my mind and my soul, and summoning them, I cry to them: O come, let us worship and fall down before Christ, our king and God."

He likens humility to *"a veil which hides from us our good deeds to keep us from the terrible sin of pride."*

"Whip your enemies with the name of Jesus, for there is no weapon more powerful in heaven or on earth."

"Solitude (hesychia) is worship and uninterrupted service of God. May the name of Jesus be united with your breath; then you will understand the value of solitude."

"When you pray do not try to express yourself in fancy words, for often it is the simple repetitious phrases of a little child that our Father in heaven finds most irresistible. . . . One phrase on the lips of the tax collector was enough to win God's mercy; one humble request made with faith was enough to save the good thief."

"The tears that come after baptism are greater than baptism itself, though it may seem rash to say so. Baptism washes off those evils that were previously within us, whereas the sins committed after baptism are washed away by tears. The baptism received by us as children we have all defiled, but we cleanse it anew with our tears. If God in His love for the human race had not given us tears, those being saved would be few indeed and hard to find."

"Let them take courage who are humbled by their passions. For even if they fall into every pit and are caught in every snare, when they attain health they will become healers, luminaries, beacons and guides to all, teaching about the forms of every sickness and through their own experience saving those who are about to fall."

"I have seen impure souls crazed for physical love; but when these same souls have made this

grounds for repentance, as a result of their experience of sexual love they have transferred the same eros to the Lord. They have immediately gone beyond all fear and been spurred to insatiable love for God. This is why the Lord said to the chaste harlot not that she had feared, but that she had loved much, and was readily able to repel eros through eros."

"If anyone could see his own vices accurately without the veil of self-love, he would worry about nothing else in his life."

Chapter **6**

Hesychasm - The Practice of Silence

The heart of Eastern Orthodox prayer teaches inner silence. Body and mind are brought to solitude and quietness in order to experience the peace and silence that surround the presence of God. The ultimate aim is a mystical union with God within a context of silence. As Bishop Kallistos Ware writes, "The hesychast, the person who has attained *hesychia,* inward stillness or silence, is *par excellence* the one who listens. He listens to the voice of prayer in his own heart, and understands that this voice is not his own but that of another speaking within him."[32]

Since solitude, or silence, is one of the rungs on "The Ladder of Divine Ascent," we shall consider it as one of the symbols to be studied in this book.

Inner Attention

Hesychia is defined as quietness, stillness, tranquility. It is one of the central considerations in the prayer of the desert fathers. It signifies not just the individual living as a solitary but the possession of inner quiet and peace. It may be used to describe not just the hermit but anyone who guards the mind, practices constant remembrance of God, and possesses inner prayer.

The hesychastic Fathers, like St. Paul, affirmed and taught that man is a Temple of the Holy Spirit. God is present within. What is needed is constant inner attentiveness to the Word of God that is constantly speaking within our hearts of the Father's infinite love for us. For this they teach the necessity of inner silence, of hesychia or resting in active self-surrender to God's love.

Hesychasm Is For All

The practice of hesychia is not just for the monk or hermit. It is meant to be practiced by all. St. Nicolas Cabasilas was a layman who lived in the 14th century. Yet he lived the same hesychastic life in the world as the monastics did in the monasteries. He described this as follows:

> *"And everyone should keep his art or profession. The general should continue to command; the farmer to till the land; the artisan to practice his craft. And I will tell you why. It is not necessary to retire into the desert, to take unpalatable food, to alter one's dress, to compromise one's health, or to do anything unwise, because it is quite possible to remain in one's own home without giving up all one's possessions, and yet to practice continued meditation."* [33]

A Prayer of Rest

The word *hesychia* in Greek also means rest. Thus the prayer of the hesychasts is a prayer of inner peace; a peace that comes from the total relinquishment of one's life to the Triune God. It is not a Utopian Nirvana-type of peace, but a peace in God in the midst of intense daily struggle. Thus, the Fathers teach us that *hesychia* or inner quietness and tranquility proceed from unceasing prayer. Hesychastic prayer leads to true rest where the soul can dwell with God in utter inner peace despite outer storms.

St. Gregory Palamas (+1359) describes hesychastic prayer as follows:

> *"Let us work with the body and pray with the soul. Let our outer man perform bodily tasks, and let the inner man be entirely dedicated to the service of God. As Jesus, God and man, commanded us, saying, 'But when you pray, enter into your closet, and when*

you have shut your door, pray to your Father which is in secret' (Matthew 6:6). The closet of the soul is the body; our 'doors' are the five bodily senses. The soul enters its closet when the mind does not 'roam' among the things of this world and the affairs of this world, but stays within — in our heart. Our senses become closed and remain closed when we do not let them be attached to external sensory things. In this way, our mind remains free from every worldly attachment; and, by secret mental prayer, unites with God its Father."

Dr. Gabriele Winckler comments on the deeper meaning of the silence that is part of hesychastic prayer:

"The hesychastic prayer teaches inner silence as the fundamental and original state of being. Hesychia is perceived as the highest realization of spiritual life, a life where body and mind are brought to absolute inner recollection and peace in order to become aware of the awesome peace and silence of which God is surrounded." [34]

Hesychia As Contemplation

Hesychastic prayer is very much like contemplation which may be defined as enjoying the Lord in silence. It is a relaxing love relationship. The mind rests and the heart is full of joy. Contemplation begins where prayer leaves off. In contemplation there are no words, no actions, no thoughts. Our heart is completely open before God. We receive His love and enjoy His presence. Contemplation, enjoying the Lord in silence, is as close to heaven as we can get here on earth. Nay, it is heaven. For, hesychastic prayer, according to Theophan the Recluse, leads us into the very presence of God: "To pray is to descend with the mind into the heart, and there to stand before the face of the Lord, ever-present, all seeing, within you."

Noise! Noise! Noise!

We live in a noisy world. The roar of traffic has grown so overwhelming that now cars are being soundproofed. And because cars are soundproofed, auto horns have to be made louder for motorists to hear them. Now we have portable transistors with earplugs constantly bombarding our eardrums with noise. An AP dispatch from Los Angeles told of a huge sixty-pound dog dropping dead of a heart attack when two smaller dogs barked at him. Noise permeates our lives. And we're paying the price.

As far back as 1927, noise was identified as a slow agent of death. Studies have repeatedly linked noise pollution not only to hearing problems but also to insomnia, ulcers, high blood pressure and heart disease.

One of the greatest needs we have is the need for silence. James Truslow Adams the American historian said, "Perhaps it would be a good idea, fantastic as it sounds, to muffle every telephone, halt every motor, and stop all activity some day, to give people a chance to ponder for a few minutes on what it is all about, why they are living and what they really want."

Intervals of Silence

A famous music master often told students that the rests were just as important in music as the notes. New students thought he was exagerating, but soon learned that without careful attention to the intervals between music phrases, however brief, the music lost half its beauty.

What is true of music is also true of life. For without daily intervals of silence and prayer, however brief, life loses much of its beauty and meaning. Even the heart that beats 70 years, rests during 35 of those years.

When the human mind is agitated, it's like the surface of the sea in a storm. No insight can emerge from the depths. But when the mind is calmed by the great hand of the Lord, then insight comes; then understanding comes; then wisdom comes. It's much like a computer. In using a computer, the operator must clear the machine of the previous problem before undertaking a new one. Otherwise, parts of the old problem carry over into the new situation, and the result is a wrong answer.

Ernesto Cardenal wrote, "Modern man always tries to flee from himself. He can never be silent or alone, because that would mean to be alone with himself, and this is why the places of amusement and the cinemas are always filled with people. And when they find themselves alone and are at the point where they might encounter God, they turn on the radio or the television set."

A Foxhole In My Mind

During the last days of World War II, President Truman was asked how he managed to bear up so calmly under the stress and strain of the Presidency. His answer was, "I have a foxhole in my mind." He explained that just as a soldier retreats into his foxhole for protection and rest, so he periodically retired into his own "mental foxhole" where he allowed nothing to disturb him.

Marcus Aurelius said once, "Men seek out retreats for themselves, cottages in the country, lonely seashores and mountains. Thou, too, art disposed to hanker after such things; and yet this is quite unnecessary, for it is in thy power, whenever Thou will, to retire into thyself. No place is quieter . . ."

It is indeed a thrill for astronauts to journey into outer space. But the greatest adventure we can make is not to the world without. It is to shut the door and enter the world within, where God waits to speak to us.

The great psychologist, William James, said once that being alone with God in prayer is much like the experience of a person who, being jostled in a crowd, climbs on a nearby doorstep, looks over the heads of the people, sees what the crowd as a whole is doing, and is then able to descend again into the jam and push; this time, not in the direction the crowd is traveling but *in the right direction*. Like a person in a telephone booth with the door open, we are bombarded daily by the many conflicting voices of the crowd. What we need is to close the door on the crowd daily and listen to the voice of God Who is trying so hard to speak to us.

Great Discoveries Made In Silence

It is in silence that some of the world's greatest discoveries have been made. Archimedes discovered the law of specific gravity while relaxing in silence in his bath. Galileo discovered the principle of the pendulum while praying silently in the cathedral of Pisa. When the scientist of today would wrest some secret of nature's mystery, he does not set up his apparatus in the midst of a noisy and crowded street, but in some quiet and remote laboratory, where he waits for nature to speak. It is so when man waits for God to speak. He must close the door on the world.

Out of the such silences have come the great prophets — Moses from the desert, Amos from the hillside, Paul from Arabia, John the Baptist from the wilderness, Anthony from the desert, and Jesus from the seclusion of Nazareth and from His forty days and nights in the wilderness.

The Mother of Prayer

Elijah found that the Lord was not in the whirlwind, nor in the earthquake, nor in the fire, but in the still small voice. It was in silence that God spoke to him. Isaiah learned that "in quietness and confidence" lay the sources of his strength. The saints and mystics of every age unite in testifying that silence is an indispensable condition of spiritual knowledge, that without it we cannot call our souls our own, that "a man does not see himself in running water but in still water," that spiritual realities do not shriek or shout but that God is waiting in the depths of our being to talk to us if we will only "wash our souls with silence." "Silence," writes St. John of the Ladder, "is the mother of prayer . . . a continuous ascension to heaven."

Jesus Practiced Solitude

Jesus practiced quietness in spite of all His activities. St. Mark, for example, tells how Jesus spent a typical day in Capernaum. Entering the town He taught in the synagogue. Then He restored health to a man with an unclean spirit. After that He went to Simon's house where He healed Peter's mother-in-law. In the evening He ministered to the sick of the city. Where did He get the strength for all this activity? St. Mark provides the answer. The next morning, he writes, "a great while before day, He (Jesus) rose and went out to a lonely place, and there He prayed." Jesus went out often to lonely places to pray. For Him they were places of power, places of strength and peace. Before His crucifixion, He poured out His soul in prayer in the lonely corner of a garden. He emerged from Gethsemane with a feeling of strength and peace. The night before He chose His own disciples He went out on the mountainside and "passed the whole night offering prayer to God."

If Jesus found it necessary to guard carefully the time for quiet and reflection, if He had to be alone to keep His soul steady, how much more do we? It is not only the health of body and soul and the state of our nerves that depend on it; something much deeper is at stake. Until we know God and are sure of Him, we have no fixed point in life, no wall, amid the pressure of things, against which to put our back. We cannot know God if we are always in motion, caught up in and held prisoners by the rush and pace of life. It is when we go into our closet and shut the door that God has an opportunity to become real to us.

God Makes Silences For Us

Perhaps this is the reason God makes silences in every life; the silence of sleep, the silence of sickness, the silence of sorrow, and then the last great silence of death. One of the hardest things in the world is to get little children to keep still. They are in a state of perpetual activity, restless, eager, questioning, alert. And just as mother says to her child, "Be still," and hushes it to sleep that it may rest, so God does sooner or later with all of us. What a quiet, still place the sick-room is! What a time for self-examination! What silence there is in a house where a loved one has died! How the voices are hushed, and every footstep soft. Had we the choosing of our own affairs we would never have chosen such an hour as that; and yet how often it is rich in blessing. All the activities of our years may not have taught us quite so much as we learned in the silences of sickness, sorrow and death. So God comes, in his irresistible way, which never ceases to be a way of love, and says, "Be still, and know that I am God."

It must be understood that silent prayer cannot stand alone. It is intimately related with public worship. As one of the saints said, *"There can be no closet prayer without common prayer."* It is common prayer that gives us the inspiration and enthusiasm to practice closet prayer.

Silence: The Mother of Knowledge

Fr. Thomas Hopko said once, "In order to pray you've got to be quiet. In order to get to know your children, you've got to be quiet. In order to get to know your spouse, you've got to be quiet. In order to get to know yourself, you've got to be quiet. In order to get to know God, you've got to be quiet.''

How few of us there are who can be still enough to hear God speak. For before we can hear Him, we must learn to go into the closet and shut the door.

Henri Nouwen writes, "We have to fashion our own desert where we can withdraw every day, shake off our compulsions and dwell in the gentle, healing presence of our Lord. Without such a desert, we will lose our own soul while preaching the gospel to others."[35]

Describing the stillness he found on the Holy Mountain, one visitor wrote:

> *This stillness, this silence, is everywhere, pervades all, is the very essence of the Holy Mountain. The distant sound of a motorboat serves only to punctuate the intensity of the quietness; a lizard's sudden rustling among dry leaves, a frog plopping into a fountain, are loud and startling sounds, but merely emphasize the immense stillness. Often as one walks over the great stretches of wild country which form much of this sacred ground, following paths where every stone breathes prayers, it is impossible to hear a sound of any kind. Even in the monastery churches, where the silence is, as it were, made more profound by the darkness, by the beauty and by the sacred quality of the place, it seems that the reading and chanting of priests and monks in the endless rhythm of their daily and nightly ritual is no more than a thin fringe of a limitless ocean of silence.*
>
> *But this stillness, this silence, is far more than a mere absence of sound. It has a positive quality, a quality of fullness, of plenitude, of the eternal Peace which is there reflected in the Veil of the Mother of God, enshrouding and protecting her Holy Mountain, offering inner silence, peace of heart, to those who dwell there and to those who come with openness of heart to seek this blessing.*[36]

The Church Fathers on Silence

"The highest form of prayer is to stand silently in awe before God" (St. Isaac the Syrian).

When Arsenius prayed, "Lord, lead me into the way of salvation," he heard a voice saying, "Arsenius, flee, be silent, pray always, for those are the sources of sinlessness."

"May the name of Jesus be united with your breath; then you will understand the value of solitude" (St. John Climacus).

"Love silence diligently for in it your soul will find life" (St. Isaac the Syrian).

"Speech is the organ of this present world. Silence is the mystery of the world to come" (St. Isaac the Syrian).

When the Fathers felt in themselves the beginning of the Fruits of the Spirit, they found their refuge in total solitude.

"I have often repented of having spoken, but never of having remained silent" (Abbott Arsenius).

The desert fathers tell of the time Archbishop Theophilus went to the desert to visit Abba Pambo. But Abba Pambo did not speak to him. When the brethren finally said to Pambo, "Father, say something to the archbishop so that he may be edified," he replied, "If he is not edified by my silence, he will not be edified by my speech."

A brother once came to visit Abba Moses and asked him for a word of advice. The old man said to him, "Go, sit in your cell, and your cell will teach you everything."

Diadochus of Photice said,

"When the sea is calm, the eyes of the fisherman can penetrate to the point where he can distinguish different movements in the depth of the water, so that hardly any of the creatures who move through the pathways of the sea escape him, but when the sea is agitated by the wind, she hides in her dark restlessness what she shows in the smile of a clear day."

"If a man cannot be alone, he doesn't know who he is," said Thomas Merton.

"Be Still and Know..."

"Be still and know that I am God," says the Lord. Be still! Stop your rushing about, all tensed up, acting as if everything depends on you, acting as if you are God. Stop! "Be still and know that I am God." In stillness as we practice God's presence, we discover who God is and who we are. The noises and disturbances of the world serve to hide our faults and our true selves from us. The desert fathers were disciples of Jesus in honest search for their true selves in Christ.

"Silence. All human unhappiness comes from not knowing how to stay quietly in a room," said Pascal.

It was Paul Tillich who said, "Language has created the word *loneliness* to express the pain of being alone, and the word *solitude* to express the glory of being alone with God."

The Place of Our Salvation

Henri Nouwen explains what happens in solitude, "Solitude is not a private therapeutic place. Rather, it is the place of conversation, the place where the old self dies and the new self is born, the place where the emergence of the new man and the new woman occurs. . . . In solitude I get rid of my scaffolding: no friends to talk with, no telephone call to make, no meetings to attend . . . just me — naked, vulnerable, weak, sinful, deprived broken — nothing. . . . The wisdom of the desert is that the confrontation with our frightening nothingness forces us to surrender ourselves totally and unconditionally to the Lord Jesus Christ. . . . Solitude is not simply a means to an end. Solitude is its own end. It is the place where Christ remodels us in His own image and frees us from the victimizing compulsions of the world. Solitude is the place of our salvation."[37]

As Mother Euphrasia, mother superior of the monastic community of Deolu of the Romanian Orthodox Patriarchate, wrote: "*Hesychia* is the supreme mark of the ascetic life and of our victory over our passions. For St. John Climacus *hesychia* is the sum of the virtues, paradise restored, heaven in our hearts. It is a different way of speaking of the gifts of the Spirit mentioned by the apostle Paul (Gal. 5:22). The hesychast possesses these gifts and exhales them in all directions like the fragrance of the knowledge of Christ (2 Cor. 2:14), as a flower gives off its scent or the sun sheds abroad its kindly light."

The Purpose of Solitude

The purpose of solitude according to the desert fathers is to descend with the mind into the heart and stand in the presence of God. It was not just a time of silence, of not speaking, but of listening to God Who dwells in the inner temple of the soul and standing in His presence.

Fr. John Meyendorff has written,

> *"Since the incarnation, our bodies have become 'temples of the Holy Spirit who dwells in us' (I Cor. 6:19); it is there, within our own bodies, that we must seek the Spirit, within our bodies sanctified by the sacraments and grafted by the eucharist into the Body of Christ. God is now to be found within, He is no longer exterior to us. Therefore, we find the light of Mt. Tabor within ourselves."* [38]

The purpose of solitude is to celebrate the liturgy in the inner chapel of the heart which is the temple of the Holy Spirit. For in reality there are three liturgies: the liturgy celebrated in the chapel of the heart for which solitude is so necessary. The corporate liturgy celebrated in church. And the liturgy after the liturgy, the *diakonia* or service rendered to Christ in the world. "I was hungry and you fed me."

Archbishop Anthony Bloom said, "It is not the desert that makes a desert father . . . the desert is everywhere." It is portable. It is within. It is solitude that creates an inner desert, an inner monastery, as it were, where we stand in His presence and where God is constantly listened to, remembered and praised.

Don't Lose Him In Your Heart

Let me share with you a folk tale from India:

"A neighbor found Nasruddin on his knees searching for something. 'What are you searching for, Mullah?' 'My key. I've lost it.' Both men got on their knees to search for the lost key. After a while the neighbor says, 'Where did you lose it?' 'At home.' 'Good Lord! Then why are you searching for it here?' 'Because there is more light here.'"

Of what use is it to search for God in holy places if you have lost Him in your heart?

Now, let us see how we can find Him in the heart so as to stand constantly in His presence.

How To Shut the Door On the World

The early church fathers speak of their private prayer life as *krypti ergasia* (secret work) or *noera meleti*. This is what they called their constant inner awareness and conversation with God. God was in the inner temple of the soul and man was in constant communion with Him. Part of this "secret work" was the recitation over and over again to onself, either quietly or more loudly, of certain prayers such as the Jesus Prayer or Scripture verses or entire Psalms.

St. John Climacus mentions this inner prayer activity when he writes, "Not even in the refectory did they (the monks) stop *noera ergasia,* but according to certain customs, these blessed men reminded one another of interior prayer by secret signs and gestures. And they did that not only in the refectory, but at every encounter and gathering."[39]

To silence the mind is an extremely difficult task. It is hard to keep the mind from thinking, thinking, thinking, forever producing thoughts in a never-ending stream. The Church Fathers have taught us the way to control the mind. It is by using one thought to rid ourselves of all other thoughts that crowd into the mind. That one thought is the Jesus Prayer. By fastening the mind on the name of Jesus we are enabled to keep the mind open to the voice of God, keeping at bay all other voices that seek to intrude.

A Time Set Apart

In order to have quiet time with God we need to set apart a time and a place to be alone with God. It could be in the early morning or late night or in the middle of the night. As Fr. Maloney writes, ". . . the living God of Abraham, Isaac and Jacob waits for us in the desert of our silent selves to reveal Himself to us in His own time and in His own words."

A successful businessman once shared his secret for preventing tensions. He had a short period of silence every day at 10 o'clock and at 3 o'clock. This did not take the usual form of prayer for he did not think about his problems but dwelt upon God's power and peace. He placed himself deliberately in God's presence and he thought of the spiritual strength of Christ flowing into him. He reported that those few minutes a day spent in God's presence resulted in complete renewal of energy and clarity of mind. "Thou wilt keep him in perfect peace, whose mind is stayed on Thee, because he trusteth in Thee," said the Prophet Isaiah (26:3).

One woman has learned to rise early each morning and spend one hour silently in the presence of God. It wasn't easy, she says. It took time and persistence to get it started. But she now feels "the warm presence of love. I know no other way to describe it. . . . Through every crisis, I have found a quietness of soul in that hour with God. It gives me time to put things in perspective, to find God in every circumstance. Once I find Him, there seems to be no problem that cannot be resolved. Because of it, my life is better. Starting my day with an hour of prayer has filled the empty space within me — to overflowing."

Other "Little Solitudes"

There are other "little solitudes" that fill our day. We can take advantage of those early morning hours in bed before the family awakens. Or the solitude of the early morning cup of coffee before leaving for work. Or the solitude of bumper to bumper traffic during the freeway rush hour. Or the solitude of waking up in the middle of the night and talking to the Shepherd instead of counting sheep. Or the solitude of a minute's silence at 6 a.m. to thank Him for the physical light of the sun and for the spiritual light of the other sun, the Son of God. At 9 a.m. to pause quietly and remember that this was the hour of Pentecost and to pray for the presence of the Holy Spirit within us. At noon to remember Jesus nailed to the cross and to thank Him for His love. At. 3 p.m. to pause and remember His death on the cross at this hour and to pray the penitent thief's prayer, "Lord, remember me when You come into Your Kingdom." And at 6 p.m. when the coming darkness reminds us of the darkness of sin and death, to remember Jesus Who came into the world as Light to destroy the oppressive darkness of sin and death.

A Silence Zone

There is no doubt that we live in a noisy world among crowds of hurrying, pushing mortals. The pressure is harder. The pace is quicker. The noise is louder. We owe it to ourselves to set up a *silence zone* somewhere in every day. When the Bible talks of one day in seven being set aside for worship, it emphasizes the need for a break in the noise. We need this break in the noise, this silent zone, every day. We need to go into our room, shut the door, and pray to our Father in secret. We need it physically; we need it mentally; we need it spiritually. Dr. Paul Tournier, the eminent Swiss psychiatrist, writes, "One day, almost a year ago, I realized I was doing myself harm because I had begun to read the newspaper before my morning meditation, the time when God was asking me to listen to Him before listening to the world. Correcting that was simple, but it was enough to brighten again the climate of my life."

Dear God
Help me to be still and know
That You are there.
I was making so much noise
That I couldn't hear You.
                        —*J. B. Turber*

The Fruit of Hesychasm

St. Symeon said of Moses, "Moses went up to the mountain as a mere man; he came down carrying God with him." St. Anthony went into the desert a mere man. He came out of it carrying God. So did the other saints. So can we if we daily descend with the mind into the heart, there to stand in God's presence. This is the fruit of hesychasm, of our solitude: to carry God into the world.

The climate of your life, too, can be brightened if you will take time to be alone with Jesus, to go into your room, shut the door against the noise of the crowd, and listen to the still, small voice of God. It speaks of forgiveness and new life. It speaks of the never-failing love of God. It speaks of security in the storms of this life and of blessed fellowship with God eternally. It speaks of peace and pardon, of courage and strength, of life and hope through Christ Jesus, our Savior. We need to pause and be silent from time to time, quietly to unwrap God's gift of life in Christ Jesus.

The whole purpose of the spiritual life is to descend with the mind into the heart through inner prayer and silence and to discover there the Kingdom of God (the grace of baptism and the Holy Spirit). The heart is the Lord's reception room. Meet Him there. "The Kingdom of God is within you," said Jesus.

Fr. Basil Pennington sums up the purpose of hesychasm:

"By deep prayer, with the help of the Holy Spirit, we can hope to so establish this deep inner quiet that even in the midst of everyday activities, this lively sensitivity will remain and all activities will be guided by the call of grace and the leading of the Holy Spirit. This is really the fruit of hesychasm." [40]

Chapter 7

Palms: Symbols of Victory, Surrender, and Allegiance

"O Lord, grant salvation! . . . Blessed is he who comes in the name of the Lord. . . . Join in procession with leafy boughs up to the horns of the altar" (Ps. 118:25-27 NAS).

Palms were used in Old Testament worship. Old Testament law (Zech. 14:16-21) directed that each worshipper entering the Temple during the seven festive days of the Feast of the Tabernacles had to carry a citron in his left hand and in his right hand a palm branch tied to myrtle and willow branches on either side. During the morning worship all the worshippers, including children, shook their palm branches toward the altar. On the seventh day, "that great day of the feast" (John 7:37) the priests made a procession around the altar seven times singing "Hosannah." Thus, this day was known as "The Day of the Great Hosannah."

―――――――――― *Emblems of Victory* ――――――――――

Apart from worship, palms were used as emblems of victory. When Simon Maccabaeus recaptured the citadel of Jerusalem in

142 B.C., "The Israelites entered it with praise and palm branches, and with harps and cymbals and stringed instruments, and with hymns and songs, because a great enemy had been crushed and removed from Israel" (I Macc. 13:51).

Palms were used also on Palm Sunday to welcome Jesus into Jerusalem as the Messiah-King of Israel. He had demonstrated His kingship by raising Lazarus from the dead. In fulfillment of Old Testament prophecies, He entered Jerusalem, the City of the King, riding on an ass' colt. He was greeted with palms and shouts of praise: "Hosannah! Blessed is He who comes in the name of the Lord! The Son of David! The King of Israel!"

Prophecy Fulfilled

The Old Testament Scripture lessons, read at the vespers of Palm Sunday (celebrated on Saturday evening), refer to the kingship of the Messiah: "Shout, O Israel, be glad and rejoice . . . the king of Israel, even the Lord, is in the midst of thee: thou shalt not see evil any more" (Second lesson: Zeph. 3:14-19). The third lesson is from the prophecy of Zachariah (9:9-15) which was fulfilled on Palm Sunday. It reads in part: "Rejoice greatly, O daughter of Zion . . . behold, thy king cometh unto thee: he is just, and having salvation; lowly, and riding upon an ass, and upon a colt the foal of an ass."

The hymns sung at the Matins or Orthros of Palm Sunday call on us to meet the King who comes to us on this day:

> *"Come, and with great rejoicing let us magnify Christ with palms and branches. . . . The Lord is God and has appeared to us; let us keep the feast together. Come, and with great rejoicing let us magnify Christ with palms and branches, and let us cry aloud. . . . We also, bearing palms and olive branches, cry aloud to Thee in thanksgiving: 'Hosannah in the highest, blessed is He that comes in the name of the Lord.'"*

Blessing of the Palms

The following prayer is used for the blessing of the palms on Palm Sunday:

> *"O Lord, our God, Who sits upon the Cherubim, Who has raised up the might of Your Only-begotten*

Son, our Lord Jesus Christ, that through His Cross and Grave and Resurrection He might save the world; and at Whose coming today to Jerusalem, unto His voluntary Passion, the people who sat in darkness and in the shadow of death, taking the symbols of victory, and the boughs of trees and branches of palms, did go forth and proclaim the Resurrection, by anticipation.

Do You, the same Lord, preserve and keep us also who in imitation of them do bear in our hands palms and boughs of trees, on this Eve of the Great Feast of Pascha.

And like unto these multitudes and children who offered unto You "Hosanna in the Highest, Blessed is He Who comes in the Lord's Name," may we also in hymns and praise attain unto the Life-Giving Resurrection on the Third Day, in the same Christ Jesus our Lord, with Whom You are Blessed, together with Your All-Holy and Good, and Life-Giving Spirit, now and forevermore. Amen."

It is important to remember that we participate in the messianic procession not only on Palm Sunday but also in every Eucharist where Christ the Messiah-King comes invisibly escorted by the Cherubim to unite Himself personally to each of us.

Symbols of Surrender

The icon of Palm Sunday shows children spreading garments on the road before Jesus. This reminds one of the twenty-four elders who cast their crowns before God's throne (Rev. 4:10). They were showing their submission and surrender. In ancient times a king captured in battle would cast his crown at the feet of the victor as if to say, "I surrender completely to you."

The branches carried on Palm Sunday were probably olive branches, common around Jerusalem. They symbolized peace, anointing, and victory. It behooves us to ask: What is the meaning of palms? Why does the Church bother to give them to us?

The meaning of these symbols is that Jesus comes to us today. Just as He entered Jerusalem on Palm Sunday, so He comes to us today in the Jerusalem of our souls. He seeks to become our personal Messiah and King. This can happen only if we offer Him our complete allegiance and surrender. Unless we surrender our lives to Jesus as Lord, He can never be *our* King. The palms are the sign of our glorification of Christ as King.

The History of Palm Sunday

The festival of the triumphant entry of Jesus into Jerusalem—which is one of the twelve principal feasts of the Church Year—began in Jerusalem, was commonly celebrated in the Eastern Church, and from there spread to the Western Church sometime between the sixth and seventh centuries, where it came to be known as Palm Sunday.

A beautiful description of how Palm Sunday was observed in Jerusalem in the fourth century is given by Silvia of Acquitaire. She visited the Holy Land as a pilgrim and described it in her Diary. The Christians in Jerusalem would re-live each year Christ's entry into the city as it originally took place. After the morning liturgy at the Church of the Holy Sepulchre, the faithful would gather at 1 p.m. in the afternoon at the Church of the Ascension on the Mount of Olives. With bishop and clergy present, as the faithful were gathering, hymns and psalms were sung. The Gospel story of the entry of Jesus into Jerusalem was read. After all had assembled, a magnificent procession began toward the walled city of Jerusalem following the path Jesus took. The procession consisted of young and old, bearing palms and olive branches in their hands, chanting hymns and psalms with the constantly recurring refrain: "Blessed is he who comes in the name of the Lord." Even infants too young to walk, carried by their parents in the procession, held palms in their hands. Finally, at the end of the procession, followed the bishop with his attendants. In imitation of Christ, the bishop rode on a donkey. Winding through the city, the procession concluded at the Church of the Holy Sepulchre with the Service of Vespers. This age-old procession still takes place today on Palm Sunday with the Patriarch of Jerusalem and the faithful following the route Jesus took. This procession marks the origin of the festival of Palm Sunday with the blessing and distribution of palms.

Faith Is Surrender

The palms and branches of Palm Sunday must remind us that the Christian faith does not consist merely in believing a certain number of truths about God. It consists primarily in surrendering ourselves body, mind and soul to Jesus as Lord and King within the context of the Church. Paul Tillich said, "Faith means being seized by a power that is greater than we are, a power that shakes us and turns us and transforms us and heals us. Surrender to that power is called faith."

When a saintly Christian was asked, "What is the first thing in knowing the will of God?" he answered in a single word, "Surrender." You cannot know God or His will unless you first surrender your life to Him.

When Jesus called His disciples, He said to them, "Follow me." That was His will for their lives. Scripture says that they left all—their homes, families, friends, businesses—to follow Him. They *surrendered* all to obey the call of the Lord.

When the rich young ruler asked Jesus, "What must I do to inherit eternal life?" Jesus asked him to surrender what he had and to follow Him—which he refused to do. The Gospel tells us that he left sorrowful.

Jesus confronts each one of us today and says, "I have done all I am going to do. I am waiting now for you to do something. I am waiting for you to empty your life of sin and self so that I can fill it. I am waiting for a fully surrendered life so that I can control it. I am waiting for a heart that is dead to everything else so that it may become alive to Me."

Refusing To Make the Great Surrender

We have a tendency to hold back. We make the small surrenders but not the great surrender, the one that can save and change our life. As E. S. Jones said, "The strangest thing on this planet is our fear of surrendering to the one safe place in the universe— God. We hug our present delusions, knowing deep down that they are delusions; but they are present, and we hug them for fear of the unknown. But that unknown is love. The earth when it runs away from the sun simply runs into the dark. When we run away from God, refuse to surrender ourselves, then we get one thing—the dark."[41]

A certain person converted and joined a small Christian church. Since they were not able to afford a custodian, every member was expected to take a turn cleaning the church. When asked to take his turn, the convert replied, "I'm converted but not that far."

That is exactly our problem. We are converted but not far enough. We have never made a complete, 100% surrender to Jesus our Lord. We are holding back. There are certain sins we have never surrendered, certain areas of life from which God is totally barred. As long as this is true, the palms we carry for Jesus on Palm Sunday are a mockery. He is not our true king.

Our Greatest Need

E. S. Jones has correctly analyzed our greatest need:

"The problem in life is self-surrender. All else is marginal. . . . Why do we fly off the handle, get angry, blow our top? Because somebody has crossed our unsurrendered self. . . . Why are we jealous and envious of others? Because somebody is getting ahead of self. All of these outer sins are symptoms of something deeper. They are the symptoms; the unsurrendered self is the disease. These are the fruit; the unsurrendered self is the root. Don't fight these outer sins. Surrender your unsurrendered self, and when you do, these outer sins will fall away, like dead leaves. . . . Yourself in your own hands is a problem and a pain, but yourself in the hands of Christ is a possibility and a power. If you will surrender yourself to Jesus Christ today, you will find yourself again, no longer a problem but a power, no longer a conflict, but a conqueror. When you belong to Jesus Christ, life belongs to you." [42]

A person who had trouble with alcohol was asked to surrender his unsurrendered self to Christ. He did. The wife came back and said to the pastor, "Thank you very much for giving my husband back to me again." The pastor replied, "I didn't give back your husband to you, he gave himself to God, and then God gave him back to himself and to you and to everybody else."

Your self in the hands of God is a possibility and a power. Your self in your own hands is a problem and a pain. Surrender to self makes life hell. Surrender to Christ makes life heaven. The more of ourselves we surrender to God, the more of our true self He gives back to us. This call to surrender is made time and again in the Divine Liturgy: "Let us commit ourselves, and one another, and our whole life to Christ our God."

Ohm's Law

There is a principle used in electricity that is called Ohm's Law. According to this principle, the amount of electricity flowing through a wire depends first upon the strength of the source of power, and, secondly, upon the resistance which is offered by the wire. If the source of power is increased, the flow of the current is increased, but if the resistance of the wire is increased, the flow of the current is decreased. This law is also applicable to our spiritual lives.

As Christians, the same God works in and through all of us. The power is the same, but the effectiveness of that power varies tremendously. Why? Because the resistance we offer to God varies tremendously. If we would only surrender our lives completely to God, offering no resistance to the Power, then God could work miracles through us. The world has yet to see what God can do with a life that is totally surrendered to Christ. Perhaps you can be that person. May the palms that you receive on Palm Sunday be an occasion for you to rededicate and surrender your life totally to the only true King—Jesus—to let His power flow uninhibited into your life.

The Obstructions

Many of us are like the inexperienced pilot who had to make an instrument landing on a cloudy day. The control tower said, "We are going to bring you in on radar." The pilot said, "That's fine." Then all of a sudden he remembered the tower, the telephone poles and the hills that surrounded the little airport, and he began to express his panic and concern about all the obstructions.

Finally, the flight controller, with a stern and authoritative command, cut in on the pilot's fears and said, "Listen, you just obey our *instructions*. We will take care of the *obstructions*."

Isn't that what God has to tell us at times? "Look, I'll take care of the obstructions. You just obey my instructions. Surrender your will to Me completely and I will lead you through the valley of the shadow of death to a safe landing at your destination."

The Difference Surrender Makes

Let me share with you a few examples of what surrender to God has meant in the lives of people.

When the angel of God appeared to Mary and told her that she of all the young Jewish women was chosen to bear the baby Jesus, she said in effect, "How? I'm a virgin." And the angel answered, "Instead of a man marrying you and you and him having this baby, the Holy Spirit is going to mysteriously overshadow you. The seed of this child will be put in your womb by the Spirit."

Now this is beyond human comprehension, even today. But this was Mary's response: "Behold the handmaid of the Lord; be it done unto me according to thy word" (Luke 1:38).

Mary was asked to do a hard thing, and sometimes God asks us to do hard things. But we can go ahead and do them if we know we don't have to do them by ourselves. We can depend on the Spirit of God to do them through us. And this is what Mary did. She simply surrendered herself to the Holy Spirit and said in effect, "Lord, just work through me. I want whatever You want to happen just as You say."

Mary gave herself to God as an empty vessel. And today we look on her as somebody really special because she did that. But when we give ourselves as vessels in whom the Holy Spirit can dwell and through whom He can work, then we are special, too, very special in God's eyes. "Whoever does the will of God," said Jesus, "is my brother, and sister and mother" (Mark 8:35). How can anyone be more special than that?

Someone said once that the Incarnation began and ended with perfect surrender to the will of God. It began when Mary said, "Be it done to me according to Thy will," and ended when Jesus said, "Into Thy hands I commend my Spirit."

A Total Surrender to God

Another example of total surrender to God comes from Mother Teresa of Calcutta. Speaking of the young "Sisters of Charity" who work with her to help the poor and dying of this world, she said,

> *"These girls wanted to give their best because in our Society (of the Sisters of Charity) we have to make a total surrender to God; this is the spirit of the community. They wanted to achieve this fulfillment in their own lives by giving all to God, giving up their position, their home, their future and dedicating all of it wholly to the poorest of the poor."*

If Jesus is God, as we believe He is, He deserves to be given everything we have, and these young Sisters of Charity make that kind of total surrender of their lives to Jesus. This is what the palms we carry on Palm Sunday should mean. "Hail Jesus! Hosannah! I accept You as my King and I surrender all to You."

A woman who had struggled with cancer for ten years surrendered her life completely to God. She wrote:

> *"I was referred to cancer specialists at Johns Hopkins University. Every three months I went for an examination. I clearly explained to them, as I had to my previous doctors, that I put neither my life nor my fate in their hands, that I had a higher loyalty in my life—the Christ within me. My body was the temple of His Spirit. I belonged to Him and nothing—not even cancer could ever separate me from His presence."*

She placed her entire life first and foremost in the hands of Jesus—her King. There is a very special kind of inner healing and peace that comes from such surrender.

From "The Imitation of Christ"

The meaning of the palms we hold is best captured by this beautiful prayer from the great devotional "The Imitation of Christ":

MY PRAYER

"O Lord, Thou knowest what is best for me, let this or that be done, as Thou pleasest.
Give what Thou wilt, and how much Thou wilt, and when Thou wilt.
Deal with me as Thou thinkest good, and as best pleaseth Thee, and is most for Thy Honor.
Set me where Thou wilt, and deal with me in all things just as Thou wilt.
I am in Thy hand: turn me round, and turn me back again, as Thou shalt please.
Behold, I am Thy servant, prepared for all things; for I desire not to live unto
myself, but unto Thee; and O that I could do it worthily and perfectly!"

Chapter 8

Good Friday: The Epitaphion and the Tomb of Jesus

The happenings of Great and Holy Friday are proclaimed in the Orthodox Church not only by word but also by dramatic action. It is one of the most beautiful services of the Orthodox worship cycle. One of the prominent symbols of Good Friday is the Epitaphion (in Slavonic, plaschanitsa), a rectangular piece of stiffened cloth on which is painted or embroidered the Body of the dead Christ laid out for burial—much like the image of Christ's Body on the Shroud of Turin.

The Epitaphion occupies an integral part of the Good Friday service because on it is inscribed the history of our salvation in blood-red letters. It speaks eloquently of God's unfathomable love. The Epitaphion itself is considered by some to be a vestige of the winding sheet in which our Lord's body was wrapped when it was laid in the tomb.

The Cross: Early Focal Point of Good Friday Worship

It is noteworthy that the use of the Epitaphion in the Good Friday service is hardly a few hundred years old. The early Christians in the Church of Jerusalem used as the focal point of their Good Friday worship not the Epitaphion but the wood of the cross which was discovered in Jerusalem by St. Helena at the beginning of the fourth century. An early pilgrim to Jerusalem, Silvia of Acquitaire (4th century), describes this rite in her Diary of a Pilgrimage. On Good Friday the bishop of Jerusalem, attended by priests and deacons, made a procession to Golgotha where a throne was set up for him on the exact spot where Jesus was crucified. Before him was placed a table covered with a white cloth on which was placed the sacred wood of the cross with its inscription. As the bishop held the ends of the cross with his hands, the faithful approached one by one, bowed profoundly before the sacred relic of the cross and kissed it.

Custom Retained

This beautiful custom of venerating the Cross on Holy Friday later spread from Jerusalem to the Orthodox Church in general where today after the reading of the fifth Passion Gospel on Holy Thursday evening, the priest takes the cross from behind the altar, carries it in a procession through the sanctuary and plants it in the middle of the soleas. During this procession, the beautiful hymn "Today He hangs on the Cross" is sung. As the following words of this hymn are sung, "We worship Thy passion, O Christ . . ." the priest, followed by the congregation, bows to the ground three times and then kisses the Precious Cross.

Origin of the Epitaphion

The origin of the Epitaphion as it is used on Good Friday is intriguing. During the Divine Liturgy, the Orthodox Church covers the sacred gifts during the proskomidi with a large veil called the "aer." The veil, also known as the "aer," began to be used in the liturgy in Jerusalem at the time of St. Savas (+532). According to Simeon of Thessalonica, the "aer" represents the naked and dead body of Jesus as it was placed in the tomb. It is for this reason, he states, that the picture of the placing of the body of Christ in the tomb is often depicted on the aer. At the Great Entrance the deacon carries the aer in a procession immediately before the Holy Gifts. When the procession reaches the holy table, the priest covers the chalice and paten with the aer as he prays silently:

"Noble Joseph took down Your most pure body from the tree, wrapped it in a clean shroud, covered it with spices and laid it in a new tomb."

From this aer or veil containing the icon of the entombed Christ, there developed slowly the use of the Epitaphion on Good Friday. The rite of the veneration of the Epitaphion was transferred from the Matins (Orthros) service of Great and Holy Saturday to the Vespers of Good Friday probably because the troparion "The noble Joseph . . ." was first sung during Passion Week in the Vespers of Holy Friday.

In addition to the figure of Christ in the tomb, there were slowly added to the icon of the Epitaphion the figures of Mary the Mother of Jesus, Joseph of Arimathea and the pious women who took part in the burial of Christ. Around the border of the Epitaphion are inscribed the words of the troparion "The noble Joseph . . ."

During the Vesper Service of Holy Friday a procession is made around the church with the Epitaphion by four persons each holding one of its four corners. After the procession it is placed in the symbolic tomb beautifully decorated with flowers and candles, while the Troparion "The noble Joseph . . ." is sung. Behind the tomb stands the plain cross with no corpus on it. The Epitaphion itself remains exposed for veneration until the Matins of the Resurrection when it is carried into the sanctuary and placed on the holy table where it is kept for forty days until the Feast of the Ascension of Jesus, to symbolize the forty days Jesus spent with us following the Resurrection.

Is God Fair?

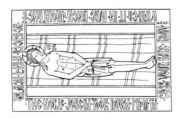

What happened on Good Friday provides the answer to a question we often ask about God's fairness and justice. St. Isaac the Syrian answered this question perceptively long ago when he wrote:

"Do not presume to call God just: for what sort of justice is this—we sinned and He gave us His only begotten Son on the Cross? Never say that God is just.

If He were just, you would be in hell. Rely only on His injustice which is mercy, love, forgiveness."

The glorious message of Good Friday is that the greatest attribute of God is not justice but mercy. It is for this reason that we plead His mercy in every worship service with the prayer *Kyrie eleison,* Lord, have mercy.

The Orthodox Attitude Toward Crucifixion As Expressed in the Hymns of the Day

Bishop Kallistos Ware writes in his book THE ORTHODOX CHURCH: "The Orthodox attitude to the Crucifixion is best seen in the hymns sung on Good Friday, such as the following:

He who clothes himself with light as with a garment
    Stood naked at the judgment.
On his cheeks he received blows
    From the hands which he had formed.
The lawless multitude nailed to the Cross
    The Lord of Glory.

"The Orthodox Church on Good Friday thinks not simply of Christ's human pain and suffering by itself, but rather of the contrast between His outward humiliation and His inward glory. Orthodox see not just the suffering humanity of Christ, but a suffering God:

Today is hanged upon the tree
    He who hanged the earth in the midst of the waters.
A crown of thorns crowns him
    Who is the king of the angels.
He is wrapped about with the purple of mockery
    Who wraps the heaven in clouds.

"Behind the veil of Christ's bleeding and broken flesh, Orthodox still discern the Triune God. Even Golgotha is a theophany; even on Good Friday the Church sounds a note of Resurrection joy:

We worship thy Passion, O Christ;
Show us also thy glorious Resurrection!
I magnify thy sufferings,
I praise thy burial and Resurrection.
    Shouting, Lord, glory to thee!

"The Crucifixion is not separated from the Resurrection, for both are but a single action. Calvary is seen always in the light of the empty tomb; the Cross is an emblem of victory. When Orthodox think of Christ Crucified, they think not only of His suffering and desolation; they think of Him as Christ the Victor, Christ the King, reigning in triumph from the Tree. . . . Christ is our victorious king, not in spite of the Crucifixion but because of it: 'I call Him king because I see Him crucified' (Chrysostom)"[43]

The Orthodox Attitude Toward the Crucifixion As Expressed In the Icon

Contrasting the Orthodox icon of the crucifixion with the stark reality of Western artists (broken bones, contorted face, bloody necks, etc.), iconographer Photios Kontoglou concludes that the latter begets despair whereas the icon breathes a message of hope. He writes:

"Here there is nothing from the world of corruption. The forms and colors do not impart the frigid breath of death, but the sweet hope of immortality. Christ is depicted as standing on the Cross, not hanging on it. His body is of flesh, but flesh of another nature, flesh whose nature has been changed through the grace of the Holy Spirit. The expression on His face is full of heavenly tranquility; the affliction which has befallen Him is full of gentleness and forgiveness, exempt from agonized contractions on the face. It is the suffering redeemer. He Who has undone the pangs of death, Who has granted the peace of the life to come. This crucified body is not that of just anyone, but it is the very body of the God-Man Himself. . . . It radiates the hope of the Resurrection. The Lord does not hang on the Cross like some miserable tatter, but it is He, rather, who appears to be supporting the Cross. His hands are not cramped, being nailed to the Wood; rather He spreads them out serenely in the attitude of supplication. . . . I repeat; the forms and colors of the liturgical icon do not express the brute horror of death, but have the nobility and gentleness of eternal life. It is illuminated by the light of hope in Christ. It is full of the grace of the Paraclete."

In some icons of the crucifixion the sun and the moon are placed in such a manner as to make it appear that the outstretched arms of the Savior are supporting them.

The Service of the Descent From the Cross

On the morning of Holy Friday the service of the Royal Hours is held consisting of Old Testament prophecies relating to the passion and crucifixion of Christ and their fulfillment in the New Testament. The Vespers for Great and Holy Friday are celebrated in the afternoon. During this service the final events of the life of Christ are retold: the trial, the sentencing, the scourging, the mocking, the crucifixion, the death, the descent from the Cross, and the burial. As the Gospel account is read, the priest, representing Joseph of Arimathea, removes the Body of Christ from the Cross, wraps it in a shroud and carries it into the altar, representing the tomb.

Toward the end of this service the priest lifts a large embroidered icon representing Christ lying in the tomb, and carries it in a procession around the church. Finally he lays it in a specially prepared tomb in the center of the church. During the procession the following hymn is sung:

"The Noble Joseph, when he had taken down thy most pure body from the tree, wrapped it in fine linen and, anointing it with spices, placed it in a new tomb."

It is around the symbolic tomb of Jesus, beautifully decorated with flowers, that the evening service takes place.

The Service of The Lamentation of Our Lord's Death

In John 19:25 we read, ". . . standing by the cross of Jesus were his mother, and His mother's sister, Mary the wife of Cleopas, and Mary Magdalene." Mary the Theotokos stood by the cross and watched her Son die. In the Lamentations that we sing on the evening of Great and Holy Friday, Mary expresses her feelings about her Son's death. Sharing these feelings we sing with her the Lamentations. Following is a sample of some of these moving stichera:

"You, who clothe Yourself with light as with a garment, were taken down from the Cross by Joseph and Nicodemus. And seeing You dead, naked and unburied, he raised a heart-rending lament and said: 'Alas, dearest Jesus! A short while ago the sun saw You hanging on the tree and covered itself with darkness. The earth trembled in fear, and the veil of the temple was torn asunder. But now I see You Who, willingly, underwent death for my sake. How can I bury You, my God? In what kind of shroud can I wrap You? With what kind of hands can I touch Your Incorruptible Body? What song shall I sing at Your departure, merciful Lord? I extol Your Passion, and with hymns I praise Your burial together with Your Resurrection,' crying out: 'O Lord, glory be to You!'"

The Procession

Good Friday in the Orthodox Church commemorates not only the death and burial of Jesus but also His descent into Hades where He preached His Gospel to all those who had died before His coming. In this descent Jesus Who is the Life encounters and destroys death. As the hymn says, "Thou hast come down to earth to save Adam, and having not found him on earth, Thou hast descended, searching him, even into Hades. . . ."

The solemn procession around the church with the embroidered icon of the entombed Christ following the Lamentations is not only a funeral procession; it is also the Son of God, the Immortal One, proceeding through the darkness of Hades pre-announcing the joy of the Resurrection. During this procession the choir sings the hymn, "Holy God . . ." The procession stops a number of times for the priest to address petitions to the Lord.

The Old Testament Prophecy
(Ezekiel 37:1-14)

The theme of the Resurrection is picked up immediately in the Old Testament reading from the Prophet Ezekiel. God speaks to the prophet who is looking into a huge valley filled with the dry bones of the dead. God announces to Ezekiel that the earth is not intended to be a universal graveyard. Not death but resurrection is the ultimate destiny of man. The dry bones will hear the words of the Lord. The dead will live again. "Behold, my people, I will open your graves and cause you to come up out of the graves . . ."

The Epistle Lesson
(I Corinthians 5:6-8; Galatians 3:13-14)

How will this universal resurrection come about? St. Paul provides the answer in the epistle lesson. "A little leaven leavens the whole lump." Christ, Who is the Resurrection and the Life, is our leaven. He is the One Who destroys death for each of us and allows us to share in His Resurrection through holy baptism.

The Gospel Lesson (St. Matthew 27:62-66)

The Gospel reminds us that the prophecy of the resurrection of the dry bones is still a prophecy not yet fulfilled. There remains one more day—Holy Saturday—before we can hear the announcement of its glorious fulfillment. So the Gospel lesson reminds us once more of the Tomb—"which was made secure by sealing the stone and setting a guard."

At the conclusion of the service it is customary in some churches for the worshippers to receive a flower from the beautifully decorated symbolic tomb of Christ. This is taken home and preserved reverently before the family icon.

"Who Loved Me..."

In the ancient world it was common that people should sacrifice to God. It is something completely new that God should sacrifice Himself for us. "It is only on a cross that a man dies with outstretched arms," said St. Athanasius. His arms were outstretched to demonstrate the unfathomable depth of His personal love for each one of us. All the world's embraces cannot compare in love with the outstretched arms of Christ on the Cross. He stands ready to embrace each one of us if we will yield our lives to Him in complete obedience and walk with Him daily. The response we are called to make to the Crucified Christ was best expressed by St. Paul when he wrote, *"I have been crucified with Christ; it is no longer I who live, but Christ Who lives in me; and the life I now live in the flesh I live by faith in the Son of God, who loved me and gave Himself for me"* (Galatians 2:20). Make Good

Friday a part of your everyday life by repeating to yourself prayerfully every morning and evening the words, *". . . who loved me and gave himself for me."*

―――――― *St. Eusebius on The Crucifixion* ――――――

"If you do not listen to Him who has created you, then ask Him who has redeemed you, how much you are worth. What is the price which Christ has paid for you? Consider His sufferings, how He was mistreated and mocked; think of the scourging, the crown of thorns, the cross. To redeem you, to purchase you, He sacrificed His life—He, God's eternal Son—He, true God like the Father. Look at the magnificence of the moon and the stars, look at the earth in all its beauty; what is it all compared to God? Hardly more than a speck of dust. Therefore, you are worth infinitely more than heaven and earth with all their splendor. The standard of your worth is the eternal God Himself, for He has purchased you with His own blood. You are worth as much as the blood of our Lord Jesus."

―――――― *St. Tikhon on The Crucifixion* ――――――

Year after year the Church confronts us every Good Friday with the great love of God in Christ Jesus. Few saints have expressed this love better than that great saint of the Russian Orthodox Church, St. Tikhon:

You lived on earth, King of Heaven, to lead me to heaven—I who had been cast out of paradise.
You were born in the flesh of the Virgin to give me birth in the spirit.
You suffered insults to silence the mouths of my enemies who denounced me
You abased Yourself, You Who are higher than all
honors, in order to honor me, the dishonored.
You wept to wipe the tears from my eyes.

You sighed, grieved, sorrowed to save me from
sighing, grieving, suffering pain through eternity,
to give me eternal joy and gladness.
   You were sold and betrayed
that I might be freed, I who was enslaved.
   You were bound that my bonds might be broken.
   You were submitted to an unjust trial—
   You Who are the Judge of all the earth—
that I might be freed from eternal judgment.
   You were made naked in order to clothe me in the
robes of salvation, in the garments of gladness.
   You were crowned with thorns,
that I might receive the crown of life.
   You were called the king of mockery—You, the
      King
of all!—to open the kingdom of heaven for me.
   Your head was lashed with a reed
that my name should be written in the book of life.
   You suffered outside the city gates in order to
lead me, one who had been cast out of paradise,
into the eternal Jerusalem.
   You were put among evil men—You Who are the
      only
Just One—that I, the unjust, might be justified.
   You were cursed, the One Blessed
that I, the accursed, should be blessed.
   You shed your blood
that my sins might be cleansed away.
   You were given vinegar to drink
that I might eat and drink at the feast in Your Kingdom.
   You died, You Who are the life of all—
in order to revive me, the dead.
   You were laid in the tomb
that I might rise from the tomb.
   You were brought to life again
that I might believe in my resurrection.''

A Good Friday Troparion

"Each part of your body suffered some outrage because of us:

Your head, the thorns;
Your face, spitting;
Your mouth, the taste of vinegar and gall;
Your ears, injurious blasphemies;
Your shoulders, the purple of derision;
Your back, flagellation;
Your hand, the reed;
Your entire body, the pangs of the cross;
Your members, the nails;
Your side, the lance.

You who have suffered for us, and who in suffering have freed us.
You who, through love of man, have lowered Yourself with us and who have lifted us up, Savior, have mercy on us."

What Does It All Mean?

The Service of the Epitaphion is truly one of the most moving worship experiences of the Orthodox Church year. It confronts us each year by word and act with Christ crucified, dead, and buried for our salvation. But the real question is: What does all this mean? What should it mean practically to those present at this service? How ought it to affect our lives? What difference should it make in our lives today that Christ died for us?

St. Paul answered these questions for us when he wrote to the Romans: "We were buried therefore with Him by baptism into death, so that as Christ was raised from the dead by the glory of the Father, we too might walk in newness of life. . . . So you also must consider yourselves dead to sin and alive to God in Christ Jesus" (Romans 6:4,11).

The two key phrases on which we shall concentrate for the meaning of Christ's death are: "DEAD to sin" and "ALIVE to God in Christ Jesus." What does it mean to be "dead to sin" and "alive to God?"

Life Is What We Are Alive To

What does being alive mean to you? It means different things to different people at different times. For Pavarotti being alive means reaching his high C. For a child being alive means licking a chocloate ice cream cone. For Alexander Fleming being alive means discovering penicillin.

When have you felt alive, gloriously alive, so brimful of life that it almost hurt? When you skimmed over the lake on skis? When you downed a mug of Budweiser on a hot, humid day? When you closed a successful deal? When someone's eyes met yours in ecstatic love? When you first laid eyes on your newborn child? What makes you feel brimfully alive?

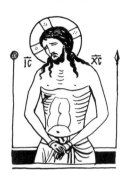

A woodsman from Wisconsin was walking on Park Avenue in New York City. Suddenly he stopped and said to a companion, "I hear a cricket."

"Nonsense," his city friend replied, "in this uproar how could you possibly hear a cricket?"

"But I do," insisted the woodsman. "Watch, I'll show you something." Taking a dime from his pocket, he dropped it on the pavement. Instantly every head within twenty feet turned around to see whose money dropped. "You see," said the woodsman, "people hear what their ears are tuned to. Mine happen to be tuned to crickets."

Life is what we are alive to. Life is that to which we have tuned the ears of our mind and heart. The student who flunks geometry because he cannot remember the theorem will remember every incident in the ball game and the batting averages of all the players. Life is what we are alive to. The man who can remember every fluctuation of the stock market for two years cannot remember the topic of last Sunday's sermon. Life is what we are alive to; what we have tuned our mental and spiritual ears to.

Alive To the Best in Life

What are we alive to? Are we alive to the highest and the best in life? Or are we alive to that which is something less, often cheap, meaningless, and base? Are we alive to the eternal? Or are we alive only to the transient and the passing?

St. Paul says that since we have died with Christ through baptism and risen with Him to newness of life, we are to be "dead to sin and alive to God in Christ Jesus." To be truly alive, he says, is to be alive to God. No one can be truly alive if one is not alive to God in Christ Jesus. But we cannot be alive to God unless we are first "dead to sin." What does it mean to be dead to sin?

Dead to Sin

A pastor was going over the church roster of members with some of his Board people. After many of the names were written the initials: FBPO. Asked to explain the meaning of these initials, he answered, "They mean 'For Burial Purposes Only.'" There are many in every church membership directory who are there in name only. They are alive to many things in life but not to God or His Church.

Albert Schweitzer said once, "The tragedy is what dies inside a man while he lives." What usually dies inside is our aliveness to God in Christ. The world exerts tremendous pressure on us each day to make us become dead to God and alive to sin. When we allow ourselves to succumb to this pressure, the result is spiritual death. Oh yes, we are physically alive but spiritually we are dead to God. The inner flame has flickered out. The most important thing within us—our aliveness to God—has died.

G. A. Studdert-Kennedy captured this state of being dead to God in a beautiful poem entitled "Christ Comes to Birmingham":

When Jesus came to Golgotha
  They hanged Him on a tree;
They drove great nails through hands and feet
  And made a Calvary;
They crowned Him with a crown of thorns—
  Red were His wounds and deep,
For those were crude and cruel days
  And human flesh was cheap.

When Jesus came to Birmingham
  They simply passed Him by,
They never hurt a hair of Him,
  They only let Him die.

*For men have grown more tender
    And they could not give Him pain—
They only just passed down the street
    And left Him in the rain.*
*Still Jesus cried, "Forgive them
    For they know not what they do."
And still it rained the winter rain
    That drenched Him through and through.
The crowds went home and left the streets
    Without a soul to see,
And Jesus crouched against a wall
    And cried for Calvary.*

One of the subtle ways by which we kill the presence of Jesus in our lives today is through this sin of indifference. It is no wonder we hear God saying in Rev. 3:15-16, "I know your works; you are neither cold or hot. Would that you were cold or hot! So, because you are lukewarm, and neither cold nor hot, I will spew you out of my mouth." A lukewarm Christian is a dead Christian, says God.

A person said once, "I wish I were dead!" And a voice from within answered, "You *are* dead. You wish you were *alive.*" Does that not describe many of us?

Consider the aimlessness of so many people today who wander from the cradle to the grave with no sense of direction or goal. Oh yes, they are busy. They are forever busy, but busy about the wrong things. They keep rushing, restlessly preoccupied, pursuing now one prize, now another—and yet, in spite of it all, they are dissatisfied, bored, unfulfilled. Is this kind of living, life, or is it death?

Oswald Chambers, the great devotional writer, talks of two funerals for each person. One he calls the "white" funeral and the other the "black" funeral. The white funeral, he says must precede the black funeral. For, the white funeral prepares us for the black funeral. The white funeral is that in which through repentance we die to our sinful self before we go through the black funeral of physical death. The white funeral gives birth to the new resurrected life which enables us to pass through the black funeral as through a door that leads to eternal life with God.

Dead Before We Die

It is not the fact of death that makes life tragic, so much as that many of us allow death to creep unto us before we die—death in the form of hardening of the mental and spiritual arteries; death in the form of forgetfulness of God and His great love for us on the cross that should be the pivotal point of our life.

Someone said, "I'm not afraid of dying, but I'm very much afraid of not living enough. I don't care how long I have, but I want to *live* all the life there is in me while I'm at it. I have only one prayer, but it's constant—'Keep me alive, Lord, while I live!'"

Keep me alive, Lord, to You, to the Cross, to Your forgiving love, to your Church, to the great privilege of being able to converse with You in prayer, to the great blessing of Your Presence which You seek to bestow upon me, to Your personal love letter to me: the Bible and the Sacraments, especially the Eucharist.

Keep me alive, Lord, to the needs of suffering humanity, and help me do something, however small, to alleviate those needs. As You did say, "As you did it to one of the least of these my brethren you did it to me."

Keep me alive, Lord; for eternal life does not begin when I die; it begins right now whenever I give my heart to You. As Phillips Brooks said, "The great Easter truth is not that we are to live newly after death, but that we are to be new here and now by the power of the resurrection." We are really raised from the dead and begin to really live the day we accept Jesus as King and Lord.

Keep me alive, Lord, *alive* to You and *dead* to sin.

Put to Death What is Earthly in You

We are to be "dead to sin," says St. Paul. Exactly what does St. Paul mean by this? What is it we are called to die to?

St. Paul answers this question clearly when he writes, "Put to death therefore what is earthly in you: immorality, impurity, passion, evil desire, and covetousness, which is idolatry. On account of these the wrath of God is coming. In these you once walked, when you lived in them. But now put them all away: anger, wrath, malice, slander, and foul talk from your mouth . . . seeing that you have put off the old nature with its practices and have put on the new nature which is being renewed in knowledge after the image of its creator" (Col. 3:5-10).

We are called to die to anger which divides and destroys, and rise to forgiveness which unites and restores. We are called to die to greedy desires to possess what is not our own, and to rise to generosity which shares its blessings with the less fortunate. We are called to die to envy of the welfare and happiness of others and rise to love which seeks to enhance the welfare of others. We are called to die to lust which would use the bodies and lives of others for ignoble ends, and rise to purity which treats others as "temples of the Holy Spirit." We are called to die to pride which places self in the place of God, and rise to humility which places God on the throne of life and makes us His joyful servants.

Crucified With Christ — Dead to Sin

St. Paul says, "I am crucified with Christ." This means that Christ died and we died with Him. Therefore we have been crucified with Christ. Christ didn't just die as a substitute for me. I am also involved in the crucifixion. The old nature in me has been crucified and put to death with all of its hopes, its ambitions, its plans, its priorities. It was nailed to the cross. We are then dead to self. "They that are Christ's," says God's word, "have crucified the flesh with its affections and lusts." In other words, the old nature, the sin nature, the self has been crucified with Christ.

St. Paul tells us that we are to reckon ourselves to be dead with Christ (see Romans 6). We are to realize that we died with Christ on the Cross, that our old nature is dead, that we are dead to the world and the world is crucified unto us, that we are dead to the flesh, that we are alive in Christ Jesus, that henceforth we are to live no more to self and sin but are to be alive unto God.

We have been dying to sin ever since our baptism. And that dying will never be ended. For, dying to sin is not something negative; it is turning to Christ which is a daily conversion. In dying to sin, we live to God.

Fr. Walter J. Burghardt explains the positive aspect of dying to sin as follows: "To the death that is sin we have been dying since our baptism. And the dying is never ended. For dying to sin is not something negative; dying to sin is turning to Christ, and turning to Christ is a constant conversion. If sin is rejection, dying to sin is openness: openness to God's presence poured out on us through every flower that opens its chaliced petals to us, every breeze that caresses our skin, every man or woman whose eyes meet ours, the awesome presence of the Holy One Himself tabernacled within us. In dying to sin, we live to God."

Move On To Growth

If ever a man experienced death to sin in all its pain and glory, it was St. Paul. Yet he did not waste his life burying that dead man who died on the road to Damascus. He boldly turned his back on him once and for all, in order that the new Christ-self that had begun to evolve in him might have room for growth. If you have died with Christ—as you have through baptism—Paul tells us, then consider yourselves dead to sin and move on to become alive to God and to share in His glory.

More Dead Than Alive

A person can be famous and great and yet live a life that is dead to the highest and the best. In his autobiography written toward the end of his life, Charles Darwin deplored the fact that he had lost his taste for music, art, and for God, too. His mind had become simply "a machine for grinding general laws out of large collections of facts," to use his own words. Whole segments of his mind had atrophied, and as a result he felt even his moral character had suffered. If he were to relive his life, he wrote, he would have set aside time at least once a week for some of the other things in life that he had neglected. To go through life being alive to the many species of life and their development but dead to the Creator of the species and the Author of all Life is to be more dead than alive. It is to miss life's greatest opportunity and privilege: to meet the Creator and come to know Him intimately in the Person of Jesus; to spend time with Him and come to know His plan for my life; nay, to let Him come into my heart and sit on the throne.

Dying to Self

A devout Christian, George Muller, writes in his "Autobiography," "There was a day when I died; utterly died . . . died to George Muller, his opinions, preferences, tastes and will; died to the world, its approval or censure; died to the approval or blame even of my brethren and friends and, since then, I have studied only to show myself approved to God."

Alive to God

Why must we die to sin? The answer is that we may be alive to God. St. Irenaeus said, "The glory of God is man become fully alive (to God) and the life of man consists in beholding God."

What does it mean to be fully "alive to God?" It means, for one thing, listening to the voice of God as Paul listened to that voice on the road to Damascus. It was by listening to the Voice that he came alive to God. God still speaks. His voice is beamed to us constantly. The problem is with us: we are not tuned in to Him.

We are tuned to other wavelengths. We miss the Voice that can resurrect us from the dead and give us life. Being alive to God means making an effort to be where God is: in the Church, in the Bible, in prayer, in the sacraments. Being alive to God means being present to Him, taking time to be silent in His presence, surrendering, putting one's spirit in tune with the Spirit of God, practicing the presence of God and deliberately seeking that Presence. Being alive to God requires "a constant aliveness to God—an aliveness present when you talk, read, watch, or examine something" (Theophan). Being alive to God means purifying the heart, cleansing it of "the lust of the flesh, and the lust of the eyes, and the pride of life" (I John 2:16) that we may see God within the heart and be alive to His Presence there. Being alive to God means seeking "the things that are above, where Christ is, seated at the right hand of God. Set your minds on things that are above, not on things that are on earth. For you have died, and your life is hid with Christ in God. When Christ Who is our life appears, then you will also appear with Him in glory" (Col. 3:1-4). Being alive to God means to "put on . . . as God's chosen ones . . . compassion, kindness, lowliness, meekness, and patience, forbearing one another and, if one has a complaint against another, forgiving each other; as the Lord has forgiven you. . . . And above all these put on love, which binds everything together in perfect harmony. And let the peace of Christ rule in your hearts. . . . Let the words of God dwell in you richly. . . . And whatever you do, in word or in deed, do everything in the name of the Lord

Jesus, giving thanks to God the Father through Him" (Col. 3:12-17).

God's Life In Us Now

Being alive to God means to have the life of God in us. Eternal life, which is the life of God, begins now, not after death. It is given to us by believing and by the living waters of baptism through which we are born anew. And this life of God or eternal life is nourished and fed by the Word of God and by the Body and Blood of Jesus in the Eucharist (John 6:51-58).

Because of our closeness to God, St. John says that Jesus is the vine, we are the branches that live from the vine (John 15:1). We are the dwelling place, the Father and the Son make their home in us (John 14:23). St. Paul says that we are a temple, and God's spirit dwells in us (I Cor. 3:16-17). So strong, so enduring, so everlasting is this life of God in us that death will never be able to destroy it. We will never cease to be branches of Christ's vine, dwelling places of God and temples of the Holy Spirit.

Powerfully Alive

Being alive to God's presence means to experience His love even in the midst of suffering. A son said to his father who had been on a bed of pain for years, "Father, I never loved you as I do now. Oh, if only I could bear your pain for you." But the father replied, "No, my son, I have not one pain left to spare. He Who allows me to suffer, loves me more than you do and knows just what is best for me. I sometimes think this is the happiest period in my life. His mercies are so great." That is to be powerfully alive to God's presence.

Dag Hammarskjold said it well: "God does not die on the day when we cease to believe in a personal deity, but we die on the day when our lives cease to be illuminated by the steady radiance, renewed daily, of a wonder, the source of which is beyond all reason."

Gilbert Chesterton said of Omar Khayyam: "The trouble with the Persian poet is that he spent his whole life in the cellar and thought it was the only room in the house."

Up From the Cellar

For many people conversion to God has meant coming out of the cellar of life, awakening to a world to which previously they had been all but dead. One day they came alive to it. One day they turned a corner, perhaps the corner of sorrow, or suffering, or trouble, and some new insight broke through to them. God became real to them. They became alive to His love, presence and power. The result was that they became new persons. They came up from the cellar of life to enjoy the gloriously beautiful sunlight of God's presence. Indeed, they became "dead to sin and alive to God in Christ Jesus."

If you are fully alive to God you will hear Jesus saying to you now through St. John Chrysostom:

> "I am father and brother and husband; I am the house, the garment, the root, the foundation-stone. I am whatever you want. If you come to me you will never lack anything; I am even ready to be your servant, for I come to serve and not to be served. I am friend and member and head and brother and sister and mother. I am everything. I have become beggar for you and wanderer for you; I went up to the Cross for you and down into the tomb for you; for you in heaven I pray to the Father and for you I came down on earth as his ambassador. You are everything to me. Brother and co-inheritor and friend and member. What more do you wish? What more can I do for you, O my people?"

The Great Mystery

The great mystery is why some Christians who are supposedly dead to sin and alive to God, while not dead, are really not fully alive. They are only half alive. Jesus does not really thrill them. His death bothers them less than their favorite actor's death. They're merely existing. They're bored, like workers on an assembly line.

The trouble with these half-alive Christians must be a weak connection of faith in Jesus. They worship at the altars of other gods. They have not fully surrendered the sinful self to Jesus. For to really believe that the life of God flows within us, like another bloodstream; to really believe that we are risen with Christ, that we are forgiven, that we can call God "our Father," that we can feed often on the flesh and blood of our Savior, this is enough to make us leap for joy as we come alive—fully alive to the joy of God's love and forgiveness.

This is what the tomb of Christ and the Epitaphion of Good Friday should signify to us: a new life, a resurrected life, brought on by a new aliveness to God and a deadness or abhorrence to sin—the sin that crucified Jesus.

Chapter **9**

The Theotokos With Child in the Apse: "Until Christ Be Formed In You"
(Gal. 4:19)

There appears in most Orthodox churches in the apse just above the holy table, a large painting of the Theotokos with the Christ Child in her bosom. The Child has an adult face to denote that even in childhood He is the "wisdom of God and the power of God."

Through the years I have met persons who have expressed dismay that the entire front wall of the sanctuary should be reserved for the Theotokos. These people believed that it should be Christ alone Who should be depicted in such a strategically important visual area. These people need to be reminded that the figure of the Theotokos with Child in the apse conveys to the worshipper a fundamentally important message, that is, it tells us what our purpose in life is as Christians. It proclaims the vitally important fact that our purpose as Christians is that Christ be formed in us (Gal. 4:19) as He was formed in the Theotokos.

Elizabeth Briere writes, "People have been heard to remark that in Orthodox churches there are often more candles lit before the icon of the Mother of God than before the icon of Christ. That observation, however, is unwittingly revealing. For the usual icon of the Mother of God does not depict her alone; it is in fact an icon of the incarnation. Venerating it, the Orthodox express reverence and awe before the humanity of God; for they see God the Word held in His Mother's arms as a baby."[44]

The Prototype of Each Believer

The Theotokos is not someone on a pedestal. She is one of us, a prototype of the true believer. She summons us to respond to the call of God with the same faith and obedience as she did in order that Christ be formed in us as He was formed in her.

Mary is the *typos* (type) of the Church, the expression of the fulfillment of the Church's mission. She is the example of the new people of God in whom and among whom God dwells: "I will live in them and move among them, and I will be their God, and they shall be my people" (2 Cor. 6:16). Mary is the fulfillment of the purpose of Christ's coming to us. He came to make us temples of the living God. "Do you not know," asks St. Paul, "that you are God's temple and that God's Spirit dwells in you? . . . God's temple is holy, and that temple you are" (I Cor. 3:16-17). As Mary became God's temple, so we are to become His temples.

My Eyes Have Seen Your Salvation

A monk of the Eastern Church wrote,

> *"Each soul ought to be a Temple of God, to which Mary brings Jesus. And each one of us should, like Symeon, take the child in his arms and say to the Father: 'My eyes have seen thy salvation.' The prayer of Simeon, 'now lettest thou thy servant depart in peace' does not simply mean that someone who has seen Jesus and has held Him in his arms can now leave this life and die in peace: it also means for us that, having seen and touched the Savior, we are released from the hold that sin has on us, and, in peace, can leave the realm of evil."*[45]

The Theotokos Speaks

Thus the figure of Mary in the apse of the church speaks a powerfully important message to us: "Look," she says, "He Who is the Lord of the Universe has become small and vulnerable for you. He comes to you utterly approachable as a Child. He desires that you take Him into your arms and into your heart and find in Him your salvation from sin and death. Look! He Who is rich, for your sake became poor so that by His poverty, you may become eternally rich" (2 Cor. 8:9).

Take this Jesus from the arms of Mary. She offers Him to you. Take Him into your arms as Simeon did. Embrace Him. Love Him. Obey Him. Follow Him. In Him you will find your peace. In Him your eyes will indeed see and experience the salvation of God.

No one has expressed the message of the Theotokos in the apse—that Christ be formed in us—better than St. Paul. His whole message centers around the indwelling Christ. One Hundred and sixty-four times in his letters he uses the expression "in Christ." No one else used this expression "in Christ." Paul invented it to indicate a totally new and completely unique experience of one who lives, yet does not live, but Christ lives in Him. For Paul says of himself, "I live, yet not I, but Christ lives in me." To the Galatians he writes, "My little children, with whom I am again in travail until Christ be formed in you" (Gal. 4:19). St. Paul was literally pregnant with Christ as was the Theotokos.

A Heavenly Ladder

Professor George A. Soteriou has written concerning the significance of the Virgin in the apse of the church: "During the Byzantine period, the allegorical meaning of the apse as a point uniting the roof of the church with the floor, and symbolically heaven with the earth, contributed to the placing of the icon of the Theotokos as Platytera. The Theotokos hovers as it were between heaven and earth as 'the heavenly ladder, whereby God has descended' and as 'the Bridge leading those on the earth to heaven'" (from the Akathist Hymn).[46] The Theotokos is not on the front wall so that we may pray to her, but with her. She is there leading us in prayer to the Pantocrator in the dome even as she holds Him as a Child. Orthodox Christians do not pray to the Theotokos.

They ask her to pray for them, to intercede to her Son in their behalf. Nowhere is this brought out more clearly than in the well-known hymn of the liturgy: "Through the intercessions of the Theotokos, Savior save us." The Theotokos intercedes. The Savior saves.

Platytera

The icon of the Theotokos in the apse is usually called "The Platytera," from the Greek (Platytera ton ouranon), i.e., "she who is wider than the heavens"—so called because she gave birth to Christ, Who as God is the Creator of all things. Having received and conceived in herself Him Who cannot be contained in the whole of creation, the Theotokos is indeed *Platytera ton ouranon,* wider than the heavens.

What Is A Christian?

What is a Christian? Many answers can be given. A Christian is a person who acknowledges that Jesus is the Son of the Living God, the Messiah, the Savior. A Christian patterns his life after the teachings of Jesus. He has been baptized. He belongs to the Church. He loves his enemies and prays for those who persecute him. He receives the Sacraments. He worships every Sunday. He has committed his life to Jesus as Lord, etc. All these definitions of a Christian are good, but they are not complete because they have left out the single most important fact about the true Christian: he/she is one in whom Christ lives. This is why the Christian life is more than *Christocentrism;* it is *Christification,* i.e., Christ living in us. To be "in Christ," says Paul, is to be united with Him, to follow Him, to be in communion with others who are in Christ through the Church.

He Lives In Me

Thus, I cannot be a Christian unless Jesus dwells in me and I in Him in the context of His Body: the Church. He breathes through all my aspirations. He wills through all my willing. He thinks through all my thinking. He loves through all my loving. He works through all my labors. The true gospel is not urging people to be good and to do good. "Try real hard to be good." That is good advice but there is no gospel in it. The true gospel is opening the door as Mary did to let Christ be formed in us, to let Him dwell within us, to forgive us, to change our personality, to liberate us, to fill us with His power, His light, His life, love and joy. It is no longer "I," but Christ Who sits on the throne of life, directing and empowering it. It is not self control but Christ control that motivates and controls life.

How important is it that we live in Christ, and Christ in us? Jesus Himself gives the answer: "I am the vine, you are the branches. He who abides in me, and I in him, he it is that bears much fruit, for apart from me you can do nothing. If a man does not abide in me, he is cast forth as a branch and withers . . ." (John 15:5-6). The real energy crisis in our world is in you and me, as we try to live the Christian life without the presence of the indwelling Christ. It can't be done. "Apart from me you can do nothing," said Jesus. That is why the Theotokos with child in the apse is the picture of every true Christian: a person in whom Jesus lives.

An Inside God

Christ is an immanent God. That is why His Name is Emmanuel: God with us. That is why the central purpose of the gospel is not only that Christ be formed in us (Gal. 4:19), but also that He may dwell in our hearts (Eph. 3:17). It is good that God is *for* us: "If God be for us, who can be against us?" (Romans 8:31). It is better that God is *with* us: "Fear thou not; for I am with thee" (Is. 41:10). But it is best that God is *in* us (Jn. 17:21). God with us. Good! God for us. Better! God in us. Best!

Although the Apostle John does not use the expression "in Christ" as Paul does, he uses the image of the vine and the branches which is much the same. The life of the vine (Jesus) is in the branches (us), enabling us to truly live and "bring forth much fruit." The secret of "bringing forth much fruit" is not toiling or spinning but abiding in Christ. Again, in the "High Priestly Prayer" in the seventeenth chapter of John's Gospel, Jesus prays that His disciples will be "in Him" and He "in them," as the Father is "in Him" and He is "in the Father." Jesus is expressing here a most intimate relationship between Himself and the believer very much like St. Paul's "life in Christ."

We Too Can Be Inseminated

We too can be inseminated by the seed of the word of God to bear the reality of the presence of Christ in our lives. When the seed of the word of God falls in the fertile soil of our heart and takes root, Christ is born within. We read in the Gospel lessons associated with the Feast Days of the Theotokos: "Blessed are the breasts that fed you." Jesus responds, "Nay, blessed rather are they who hear the word of God and keep it."

This is not a put-down for the Theotokos. She is totally one of us. What she did, we are called to do: to hear the word of God and keep it. That was her mission and ours!

Other gospel readings on the Feast of the Theotokos tell the story of those who said to Jesus: "Your mother and brothers are here!" Jesus responds: "Everyone who hears the word of God and does it is my mother and brother and sister."

St. Ambrose expressed it well: "Every believing soul conceives and gives birth to the Word of God; Christ, by means of our faith, is the fruit of us all, thus we are all mothers of Christ." The same Christ comes to be born in us and to dwell in us even as He did in the Theotokos.

A Christ Not In Us Does Not Save

A famous spiritual writer said once, "This is the whole Gospel, the birth of the holy Jesus within us; His conquering life overcoming our inward death. A Christ not in us is a Christ not ours." It is much like two persons who have a deadly disease for which only penicillin is the cure. Both say they believe in penicillin. However, one takes it; the other does not. One survives, the other does not. "A Christ not in us is a Christ not ours." A Christ outside us will do us no good. It is the Christ inside who saves and empowers.

In the World But Not Of the World

Christ commands us to be *in* the world but not *of* the world. We cannot help being *in* the world. We have no choice. We were placed here by God. But to be *of* the world is our own moral choice. We don't have to be *of* the world. Those who are *of* the world are pushed around by forces too big for them to resist. But those who are *in Christ* instead of *of the world* are not pushed around. The Presence of Christ within gives them the grace and power they need to live victorious lives. They are *in* the world but not *of* the world because they are *in* Christ. P. T. Forsyth said it well: "Unless there is within us that which is above us, we shall soon yield to that which is around us."

A New Creation

Christianity is not primarily the following of a code or rules. It is first and foremost the invasion of our lives by an altogether new quality of life which St. Paul calls *kainotis zois,* newness of

life, a totally new quality of life, a supernatural quality which is nothing else than the life of Christ Himself. So new is this life that Christ infuses in us that Paul calls it a "new creation": "Therefore, if any man is in Christ, he is a new creation; the old has passed away, behold, the new has come" (2 Cor. 5:17). Just as we cannot live at all physically unless the air is in us and we are in the air, so for the Christian Jesus is the atmosphere of life. He is always conscious of that presence and cannot live without it. The astronauts can not survive a moment in outer space without their space suits in which they carry with them the atmosphere of the earth. So the Christian carries with him wherever he goes the atmosphere of Christ. He lives and breathes in Him. "I live, yet not I, but Christ lives in me."

Paul says of Christ in us that He is "the hope of glory." "Christ in you, the hope of glory" (Col. 1:27). He is the One Who illumines all our thinking, the deepest motive of all our decisions, the nerve of all our moral courage, the One Who destroys our sin and death to enable us to share in the eternal glory of God. Not Christ *outside* but Christ *in* you, the hope of glory."

An Indwelling Christ

If Shakespeare lived in you, you could write great poetry. If Handel lived in you, you could compose magnificent music. If Christ lived in you, you could live a great life. But there is no *if* about it. You cannot have an indwelling Shakespeare or Handel, but you *can* have an indwelling Christ. This is what enabled Paul to say, "I can do all things through Christ Who strengthens me" (Phil. 4:13), not "some" things but "all" things. Who did more for Christ than St. Paul? Even though he was not one of the original twelve disciples, he traveled more missionary miles and reached more people for Christ than any apostle who had been with Christ. He did this through the power of the indwelling Christ. Truly ". . . he who is in you is greater than he who is in the world" (I Jn. 4:4).

The Example of The Martyr Felicity

Let me share with you what the indwelling Christ meant to the early Christian martyrs. A group of Christians faced martyrdom in the arena at Carthage in the year 203. Among them was a slave girl, Felicity, who was pregnant, and who therefore would not be executed until she had been delivered first of her child. Her companions offered prayer on her behalf, and immediately the birth pangs came upon her. At this point we read in the *Acts of the Martyrs:*

> *"She suffered a good deal in her labour because of the natural difficulty of an eight month's delivery. Hence one of the prison guards said to her: 'You suffer so much now—what will you do when you are tossed to the beasts? Little did you think of them when you refused to sacrifice.' 'What I am suffering now,' she replied, 'I suffer myself. But then Another will be inside me who will suffer for me, just as I shall be suffering for him.'"*

Christ was indeed an indwelling presence and power in Felicity's life. How else can we explain her remarkable courage to confess Christ so bravely in the face of death? The same Christ craves to dwell in you as He dwelt in the Theotokos and as He dwelt in Felicity, to give you the same courage and strength to do all things in Him.

How Is Christ Formed In Us?

How do we receive the life in Christ about which we are talking? How can the Christ become a reality in our lives? How is He formed in us?

Our life in Christ comes as we are baptized into His body, the Church. It is through baptism that we first "put on Christ." As St. Paul writes, "As many of you as have been baptized in Christ have put on Christ" (Gal. 3:27). In other words, life in Christ is not simply a mystical relationship between Christ and the individual believer, but is objectively based upon the believer's membership in the Church which is the visible Body of Christ. The Christian is not called first to an "imitation of Christ" but to life in Christ, since there can be no imitation of Christ unless Christ Himself dwells within us. As Nicholas Cabasilas emphasizes there can be no life in Christ except through baptism, chrismation, and the eucharist.

The Eucharist

As Baptism is the sacrament of "newness of life," so Holy Communion is the sacrament of life in Christ. As our Lord emphasized, "He who eats my flesh and drinks my blood abides *in* me and I *in* him" (John 6:56). St. Symeon the New Theologian had a vision of the life of Christ in him after he came back from church one day where he had received Communion. He looked at his hands so frail, so powerless and saw in them the hands of Christ. He looked at his body so old, so decaying and saw in it the dwelling place of Christ. For he had just received the Precious Body and Blood of Jesus. He wrote in his "Divine Hymns of Love," "We become Christ's limbs, or members, and Christ becomes our members. . . . Unworthy though I be, my hand and foot are Christ. I move my hand, and my hand is wholly Christ, for God's divinity is united inseparably to me. I move my foot, and lo! it glows like God Himself . . ."

Nurtured By Faith

Although the life in Christ is given to us as a gift of God's grace through baptism, chrismation and the eucharist, it must be nurtured by faith. St. Augustine pointed out many centuries ago that what is remarkable about the Theotokos is not that she conceived Christ in her flesh: "Mary was more blessed because she laid hold of faith in Christ than because she conceived the flesh of Christ. . . . Her motherly relationship to Him would have been of no use to Mary had she not carried Christ in her heart more happily even than she carried Him in her womb."[47]

A Personal Faith

Mary's faith said yes to God's request. Our faith, too, must say yes to Him before Christ can be conceived in us. This means that the faith that my parents and godparent confessed for me when I was baptized as an infant must now be confessed personally and consciously by me. It must become *my* faith. This is something we are invited to do in every liturgy when we are called upon to confess the Nicene Creed. We are confessing personally and publicly our Christian faith. This is why we must not do it by rote or cursorily but with all of our mind and heart in it.

In addition to the liturgy, our confession of faith is renewed daily in our private prayer life as well as in the prayers of the Church.

The figure of the Theotokos with child in the apse of the Orthodox Church reminds us that our purpose in life is that Christ be formed in us. She shows us that a Christian is one in whom Christ lives. She invites us to receive within us by faith, by the word of God and by the eucharist the Christ Who was conceived and formed in her that we, too, may become THEOFOROI, i.e., "God-bearers," offering the dying world a real Christ incarnate and living in us. She stands before all of us on the front wall of the church to lead us in prayer to her Son, the Pantocrator, in the dome. Completely one with us, she is the first to experience theosis, to become by grace what God is by nature. Like a ladder, she unites heaven and earth; for it was through her that God in Christ came to us, and by faith, like Mary, we too may ascend to Him.

The Next Step In Evolution

C. S. Lewis said, "People often ask when the next step in evolution—the step to something beyond man—will happen. Well, on the Christian view, it has happened already. In Christ, a new kind of man appeared; and the new kind of life which began in Him is to be put in us."

This new kind of life came first to Mary as she said Yes to God. This is indeed the next step in the evolution of man. For when man receives Christ within, he receives a new quality of life, the life of God, and human nature becomes transfigured "from glory to glory" to use St. Paul's expression.

I conclude with this story.

A new pastor had come to a village and called at a certain cottage. When the husband came home from work, the wife said, "The new pastor called today."

"What did he say?" asked the husband.

"Oh," she answered, "he asked, 'Does Christ live here?' and I didn't know what to say."

The man's face flushed. "Why didn't you tell him we were respectable people?" he asked.

"Well," she said, "I might have said that, only that isn't what he asked me."

"Then, why," pursued her husband, "didn't you tell him that we said our prayers and read our Bible?"

The wife replied, "But he didn't ask me that."

The man grew more vexed. "Why," he continued, "didn't you say that we were always at church?"

The poor woman broke down and said, "He didn't ask that either. He asked only, 'Does Christ live here?'"

Every time we come to church to worship, the Theotokos in the apse, with Christ in her bosom, asks the same question of each of us, "The Christ Who lived in me, does He live in you?"

> I AM INADEQUATE
> without Christ Who gives me power.
> I AM INSENSITIVE
> without my Lord Who makes me see
> and feel another's hurt.
> I AM ALONE
> if I try and walk the path myself.
> I AM POWERLESS
> if I believe I can do it
> on my own strength alone.

I AM DESTINED TO LOSE
 if it is only for my own sake
 that I live this life.
I WILL FAIL
 should success be my only criterion
 for living.
I WILL STUMBLE
 unless God shows me the way.
I REMAIN NOTHING
 until God uses me for something.
COME, DIVINE SON, MAKE YOUR HOME
 IN ME.   AMEN.

Chapter 10

Christ Pantocrator

One of the most typical and most meaningful symbols of our Church is the icon of Christ Pantocrator, the Lord Omnipotent, that appears in the dome of most Orthodox Churches. It is the image of the glorified Christ reigning on His heavenly throne.

In the catacombs, the underground tombs where the early Christians worshipped, Christ was depicted as the Good Shepherd Who protected His flock. In an age where the Huns, the Vandals, and the Mohammedans threatened the very fabric of the newly established Church, the early Christians needed an emphasis on the Almighty God Who sat enthroned as Emperor, Monarch, Ruler, surrounded by His heavenly court of saints and angels and Who dominated His flock. It is something similar to the emphasis we find in the beautiful hymn:

"This is my Father's world:
Though the wrong seems oft' so strong,
He is the ruler yet."

Based On "Revelation"

The word "Pantocrator" and the idea behind it appear in the book of Revelation. We hear God saying in Rev. 1:18, "I am the Alpha and the Omega, saith the Lord Who is, and Who was, and

Who is to come, the Pantocrator (Almighty)." The use of the multi-colored band that we usually see around the figure of the Pantocrator in the dome is based on Rev. 4:3 where the iris or rainbow is said to surround the throne of God ". . . and round the throne was a rainbow that looked like an emerald."

Normally, the icon of Christ Pantocrator is the most remote of all the conventional poses, Christ is distant from us, and sometimes His face is stern. Yet in Serbia we find an icon of the Pantocrator with dancing eyes. His face is sharp, His mouth tiny with the effort of suppressing a smile, his fingers thin and dancing, where they hold the book. The Gospel book is closed, but Jesus knows what is inside: the good news of God's love, of the destruction of sin and death, of life everlasting. hence the smile on His face.

The Entire Church Present

It is noteworthy that the highest point of the Church is reserved for our Lord. His Mother and all the other saints, angels and prophets are depicted on the walls immediately below the Pantocrator. Finally, the floor level of the Church is reserved for us— the members of the Church militant. Thus around the figure of Christ in the dome is gathered His entire Church both that in heaven as symbolized by the saints in the icons and that on earth as expressed by the presence of the living members. This gives expression to our faith that at each liturgy, the entire Church is present; those who have passed on into the other life as well as ourselves. That is why we take the opportunity to remember our departed loved ones in memorial prayers. As part of the Church Triumphant they are present at each liturgy, where the entire Church— that in heaven and that on earth— merges and comes together to glorify and sing praises to the Risen Christ, the Pantocrator.

Victory of Christ

The figure of the Pantocrator in the dome serves to express also the victory of Christ's Resurrection which is so central to our Orthodox Christian faith. It is to dramatize this victory that the figure of Christ is placed at the highest point of the Church, giving full expression to the great victory hymn of the early Church as quoted by Paul in his letter to the Philippians: "He (Jesus) emptied Himself taking the form of a servant . . . and became obedient unto death, even death on a cross. . . . Therefore God has highly exalted Him (lifted Him up) and bestowed on Him the name which is above every name, that at the name of Jesus every knee should bow, in heaven and on earth and under the earth, and every tongue confess that Jesus Christ is Lord, to the glory of God the Father" (Phil. 2:7-11).

His Eyes Upon Us

One of the reasons the Pantocrator is suspended over us in the dome is to remind us of His all-pervading presence in the universe as we come to worship Him. His presence, especially in Church, hovers over us as we pray together. He hovers above us listening to our prayers. Just as a mother cannot take her eyes off her children, so His eyes are upon each of us. He looks down and sees not only who is present in the congregation but also who is absent. One of His greatest heartaches must be to see how many of His children do not come to be with Him on His day, *Kyriaki,* the Day of the Lord. On any given Sunday more than two-thirds of His people are absent from worship. How many times He must have heard all the lame excuses I so often hear as a priest: "I may not come to Church, but I worship God at home every day." I cannot imagine a person who really worships God at home every day, *not* coming to church on Sunday to be with his Lord, to consummate his love by receiving Jesus in the Sacrament of Communion. We worship God truly not only with our tongue but also with our feet. If our heart is in the right place, it will propel our feet each Sunday to be in the right place.

I have discovered that the easiest person in the world to deceive is ourself—and the devil really helps us here. There are people who think they are still Christians when they seldom if ever come to the liturgy on Sunday, seldom if ever receive His precious Body and Blood unto forgiveness of sins and life everlasting.

"Let Us Lift Up Our Hearts"

As I look up at the Pantocrator Christ each Sunday in the liturgy when I say the words, "Let us lift up our hearts," the thought comes to me that I am always only a heartbeat away from appearing before Him in person. I think of the Second Coming and Judgment Day when I shall appear before Him to give an account of my life. It is a very sobering experience; an experience that helps me practice the presence of God all week long. I don't get this if I stay home on Sunday. In fact, if I stay away long enough, I forget God altogether. Other things begin to take His place in my life. I become spiritually dead, alive to the world and dead to Christ.

How Great!

The Pantocrator Christ serves to remind us of the majesty and greatness of God. In fact, as one gazes at the Pantocrator in the dome, one cannot fail to be impressed by the great power and magnificence suggested by His neck and shoulders. Some years ago a person visited the observatory atop Mt. Wilson in Southern California. On the wall was a picture of a star. The following words were written beneath the star:

"The light of this star began its journey toward earth 30,000 years ago. It only recently reached this planet and was photographed for the first time at Mt. Wilson."

Almost breathtaking: travelling at 14 billion miles per day! And it took 30,000 years to arrive! And who made that star? Who else but the Pantocrator!

The same God Who made the stars holds in His hand every breath we draw (Dan. 5:23). *Pantocrator!*

A great preacher said just before he died, "We have preached a great gospel, but remember Jesus Christ is greater than anything we have ever said about Him." *Pantocrator!*

We Go To Where We Belong

Each Sunday, as God's people, we gather around the One Who loves us. Each Sunday we come to Him to Whom we belong. We gather in the place where we belong: in Church under His Presence. If we do not come to church, we are acknowledging that we do *not* belong to Him. We may belong to money, to golf, to fishing, to hunting, to football, to TV. We may belong to the world, but not to God. We come to church each Sunday to acknowledge whose we are and where we belong. Just as at the end of each day we go to where we belong—home—so on the Lord's Day we go to where we belong— the Church. We gather to worship and bow the knee and the heart to the Pantocrator. This is why Jesus said that at the Resurrection there will be a separation of the lambs from the goats, i.e., people will gravitate to where they have always belonged, either toward the presence of God or away from the presence of God, either toward heaven or hell.

A father was out in a potato patch late one night to steal potatoes. He looked to the right, to the left, forward and backward and seeing no one, he was about to start filling his sack when his little son who was with him said, "Dad, you forgot to look up."

Erasing The Videotape

How often we, too, forget to look up. We forget that there is Someone Whose presence hovers over us not just when we come to church but constantly. The King—the Pantocrator—is always in the congregation. One day we shall all appear before Him and He will play for us a videotape of all that we have said and done in life. How would we like to see on videotape in God's very presence all of our sins and hear all the terrible words we have spoken. For some of us it will be a moment of extreme embarrassment that will lead to eternal separation from God. But God in His great love for us died on the cross and was resurrected to forgive our sins and cleanse us from all unrighteousness. He calls on us now to repent of our sins so that those embarrassing episodes may be completely erased from the videotape of our lives, so that we may appear before Him with a clean tape, cleansed and washed by the Blood of the Lamb.

The Meaning of God's Seeing

The Pantocrator Christ in the dome of the Orthodox Church serves to remind us that God's presence constantly hovers over us no matter where we go. We can never escape His presence. He sees us not because He wants to catch us doing something wrong in order to punish us, like the ever-present video cameras in the banks. He watches us because He loves us. As a mother cannot take her eyes off her newborn baby, so the Lord does not withdraw His eyes from those who put their trust in Him (Job 36:7).

Romano Guardini captured so well the meaning of God's seeing, as expressed by the icon of the Pantocrator in the dome, when he wrote,

> *"God is He Who sees. But His seeing is an act of love. With His seeing He embraces His creatures, affirms them, and encourages them. . . . His seeing is not the kind that merely looks at something: it is creative love, it is the power which enables things to be themselves and rescues them from degeneration and decay. . . . God turns His face to man and thereby gives Himself to man. . . . To be seen by Him does not mean being exposed to a merciless gaze but to be enfolded in the deepest care. . . . We are seen by Him whether we want to be or not. The difference is whether we try to elude His sight, or strive to enter into it. . . . None of the shortcomings and evil in our lives are fatal so long as they confront His gaze. The very act of placing ourselves in His sight is the beginning of renewal. . . . But everything is in danger once we refuse to place ourselves and our lives in His sight."*

Thank God, then, that the eyes of the Pantocrator are constantly upon us. He sees us in our sorrow to comfort us. He sees us in our grief to uphold us. He sees us in our sin to forgive us if we repent. He sees us with love and it is His seeing that keeps us at our best. If the eyes of Christ are windows through which God sees us, they are also mirrors in which we see ourselves as cared for and loved by our Creator and Redeemer.

A Defenseless Church Against An Empire

The image of Christ Pantocrator was greatly emphasized by the Apostle John in the Book of Revelation and for very good reason. When John was exiled on the Island of Patmos, his exile was due to the fact that the mighty Roman Empire had begun a massive persecution against the early Christian Church in order to crush it. The times were ominous. No one had ever withstood the invincible power of Rome. How could these poor, humble, defenseless Christians survive against such might? John provides the answer in the Book of Revelation. They will survive because of God.

In Control of Everything

God is not weak. He is Pantocrator, which means literally *in control of everything*. Whereas the word *Pantocrator* is used only once in the New Testament, it is used eight times in the Book of Revelation. The persecuted, suffering, bleeding, decimated Church will survive, says John, because God is still on the throne. It was as if he were saying to the beast which is the Roman Empire, "You do not have the last word. You are not in control. God has the last word and He is in control." "Hallelujah! For the Lord our God the Almighty reigns" (Rev. 19:6). The picture of Christ painted by John in the Book of Revelation is the picture the suffering Church needed at that time. It was the Lord Jesus, risen, ascended, sitting on the throne of glory, able and willing to save His people against impossible odds. With that kind of a Christ, a person could face situations that would drive a person without Christ to utter despair.

As Metropolitan Emilianos Timiadis has written:

"Christ reigns. He is on the throne. All through the Bible we notice that when the seers of God were in trouble they saw . . . a throne. Ezekiel in exile saw a throne. Daniel surveying 'the abomination of desolation' saw a throne. John, a refugee on Patmos, saw a throne. In all of the darkness of their times, the martyrs saw a throne. This world is not ours. Nor does it belong to the evil powers of the Devil, although it seems like it does at times. It is God's world; Christ reigns. He has overcome the world."[48]

The Old Testament Fulfilled

In the Old Testament the message was that God would be victorious in the battle with evil. He would raise the dead. The new age, eternity, would burst upon us. A new heaven and a new earth would come into being. At the end of days God would send the Messiah and appoint Him King and Judge, Pantocrator.

In the coming of Jesus all of this was fulfilled. The Messiah came. He was raised from the dead "the first fruits of those who have fallen asleep" (I Cor. 15:20). In Him salvation has come; sin is forgiven; death is destroyed; new life has begun; the Spirit is at work. "The Lord God the Almighty reigns."

A Two-Level View

John saw visions in the Book of Revelation. Through these visions God was showing him what the real situation was during those terrible persecutions that took the lives of millions of Christians. Rome may be trying to destroy the Christians down below, but God was still on His throne upstairs. Never lose sight of God, John was saying. It was like a two-stage theater. Some things were happening upstairs that clarified what was going on downstairs, even though the people downstairs could not see it. John was trying to get the early Christians to look up to see the Pantocrator Christ. It was not just what the Roman Empire was doing downstairs in its efforts to crush the Church that represented reality. God Omnipotent was still upstairs, still reigning, still in control. Ultimately, the Roman Empire would destroy itself and the Church would survive. This was the greater reality.

We need this kind of double vision as we go through life: to keep one eye on what is going on upstairs and another eye on what is going on downstairs, to see and never to lose sight of the Pantocrator, Omnipotent, sitting on the Heavenly Throne, in control of everything. Thomas a Kempis put it this way:

"The sons of God, standing on things present, do contemplate those things that are eternal. They look on transitory things with the left eye, and with the right (eye) do behold things of heaven."

Upstairs/Downstairs

To become so absorbed with what's happening downstairs so that we forget Who is in control of everything upstairs is to lose our soul.

No matter what happens downstairs, God is still on His throne upstairs as King of kings and Lord of lords. We must never lose this "double vision" that we have as Christians. We must never look only at what is happening downstairs without seeing at the same time the beautiful vision of the Pantocrator upstairs. This is what restores our balance and gives us the true perspective on life. The dangers and the threats will always exist. The doctor will continue to say that there is going to have to be a dangerous operation. The politician will continue to talk of the danger of an economic collapse. The prophets of doom will continue to speak of a coming nuclear holocaust. But as Christians we do not lose hope, because God opens our eyes to see the total reality of things, i.e., that He is still on His Throne. He still rules as Pantocrator and King. His eye is upon me, He keeps me in the center of His love and care as I keep Him in the center of my love and obedience.

The Fourth Chapter of Revelation

The heavens opened for the apostle John at Patmos and he saw the glorious vision of God seated on His throne. It was a vision John needed because he was exiled on Patmos for his faith at a time when the Christian Church was being persecuted mercilessly by the mighty Roman Empire. But God showed John through this vision that it was not the Roman Empire that was almighty but God. I wish you would take the time to read the entire fourth chapter of the Book of Revelation where John describes his vision of the throne of God. Let me quote just briefly from it:

> *"At once I was in the Spirit, and lo, a throne stood in heaven, with one seated on the throne. . . . From the throne issued flashes of lightning, and voices and peals of thunder, and before the throne burn seven torches of fire . . . (and there is) a sea of glass, like crystal. . . . And the four living creatures, each of them with six wings . . . never cease to sing, 'Holy, holy, holy, is the Lord God Almighty, Who was and is and is to come!' . . . And whenever the living creatures give glory and honor and thanks to Him Who is seated on the throne, Who lives forever and ever; they cast their crowns before the throne, singing, 'Worthy art Thou, our Lord and God, to receive glory and honor and power, for Thou didst create all things, and by Thy will they existed and were created.'"*

The Pantocrator in the dome seeks to express this vision of the All-powerful God enthroned in glory as envisioned by the Apostle John at Patmos. "Then I saw a new heaven and a new earth . . . and He Who sat upon the throne said, 'Behold, I make all things new'" (Rev. 21:1,5).

The Early Christians

The faith expressed by this vision of God on His Throne was the faith of the early Christians. We hear them say in Acts 4:24-26,

"Sovereign Lord, who didst make the heaven and the earth and the sea and everything in them, Who by the mouth of our Father David, thy servant, did say to the Holy Spirit, 'Why did the gentiles rage and the peoples imagine vain things? The kings of the earth set themselves in array, and the rulers were gathered together, against the Lord and against His Anointed.'"

According to the Psalm from which the apostles quoted, this is what happens upstairs when we rebel against God's authority,

"He who sits in the heavens laughs; the Lord has them in derision. Then He will speak to them in His wrath, and terrify them in His fury, saying, 'I have set my king on Zion, my holy hill'" (Psalm 2:4-6).

How much we need today the faith of this vision of God on His throne. No matter how hopeless the situation may seem in our lives, even when we feel we have come to the end of our rope, God is still on His throne. He is still the supreme ruler of His world. Nothing can ever defeat Him. If we cooperate with Him, He will bring about a glorious victory of truth and righteousness in our lives. He will see to it that "all things work together for good to those who cooperate with Him." Ultimately He will reign. All His enemies "shall be under His feet" and "before Him every knee will bow."

Obscuring the Vision

Satan tries constantly to obscure this vision of God on His throne through discouragement and despair. When the iconographer was painting the Pantocrator on our dome, he erected scaffolding with a platform under the dome. The ceiling of the church was made low and heavy. The atmosphere was oppressive. But when the platform was removed and we could see the beautiful vision of the Pantocrator on His throne, everything changed. The ceiling of life was lifted. We could see the One Who was in charge of the universe, sitting on the throne.

How easy it is to lose one's poise and balance as one beholds the terrible things going on in our world. The easiest way to falter is by looking only at what's going on downstairs, to forget to look upstairs to see that the world has not gotten out of God's control. He is still on the throne.

Is He Really On the Throne?

I remember descending the steps of a cave in Bethlehem and coming to a place where one could see the countless little bones of the innocent infants whom Herod the king had killed when he learned of the birth of Jesus. In his effort to destroy Jesus, he ordered the slaughter of all the children who were two years and younger. When we read of tragedies like this, we begin to wonder whether God is really on His throne.

Some time ago the TV movie "The Day After" depicted how millions upon millions of persons would suffer and die in the event of a nuclear war. Many of them would be innocent children. As we live with the possibility of such a tragedy, we begin to wonder if God is really on His Throne.

He Will Have the Last Word

This is why we need the Church and the Bible. It is only here that we get the real message. There is a Throne. "The Lord God omnipotent reigns." He is not dead. He is not sick. He is not weak. He has not abdicated. He is alive and well. The kings and the mighty who persecute the innocent and cause their suffering and death will come before God's Throne to give an account of their actions and be judged. God's justice will triumph for eternity. The innocent will be resurrected to enjoy the crowns of their martyrdom. The guilty will also be resurrected to suffer the punishment for their evil deeds. The last chapter of our lives will be written in heaven. Not evil, not injustice, not dictators, not nuclear holocausts, but God Almighty, the Pantocrator, will have the last word. He is on the Throne. "The Lord God omnipotent reigns."

The Great Victory

The icon of the Pantocrator reminds us that the Almighty God Who sits on the Throne has accomplished for us the greatest victory this universe has ever seen: the Resurrection.

Because of our Lord's resurrection, the true Christian is an eternal optimist. The trouble with being an optimist is that people think you're naive; you don't know what's really going on. The real Christian is anything but naive. He knows that there are evil persons in the world who want war. He knows there are such things as cancer and multiple sclerosis. But He remains an optimist because he knows that in Christ he holds the winning ticket in a cosmic sweepstake. He does not look only at what is going on downstairs. He looks upstairs at the One Who sits on the Throne; the One Who said, "In the world you have tribulation; but be of good cheer, I have overcome the world" (Jn. 16:33).

As one Christian said, "If I am in Christ, I am not in a defeated Christ; I am in a Christ Who wrought the greatest victory ever seen on our planet—the victory of life over death—and wrought it not only for Himself, but also for those who believe in Him that they may have the power to walk out of a dead past into a triumphant future."

Every time we come to church and look up at the Pantocrator we think of the great victory He won for us and we claim that victory. It is of this victory that St. Paul sings in Romans 8:35-39:

"We are more than conquerors through Him Who loved us. What can separate us from the love of Christ? Can affliction or hardship? Can persecution, hunger, nakedness, peril, or the sword? 'We are being done to death for thy sake all day long,' as Scripture says; 'We have been treated like sheep for slaughter'—and yet, in spite of all, overwhelming victory is ours through Him Who loved us. For I am convinced that there is nothing in death or life, in the realm of spirits or superhuman powers, in the world as it is or the world as it shall be, in the forces of the universe, in heights or depths—nothing in all creation that can separate us from the love of God in Christ Jesus our Lord."

Unapproachable?

Sometimes as we look at the Pantocrator Jesus in the dome in all His divine glory and power, we may be tempted to think that

He is far removed from the world, reigning as Lord, but somewhere way up in the sky. The great temptation through the ages has been to doubt not the divine nature of Jesus but His humanity, to adore Him so greatly as to lift Him straight out of real life into some kind of "other worldly" world. In fact, one non-Orthodox Christian said of the Pantocrator Christ that "He is depicted as the stern Judge before whose awful righteousness one may fall and worship but to whom one is unlikely to come in trust, with love and gratitude."

But we must remember that this Pantocrator Jesus in the dome did not stay up there. He "came down from heaven for our salvation and became man" as the Nicene Creed says. He became a real person like you and me. In fact, He was so common that Mary Magdalen mistook Him for a gardener. How could anyone have become more commonplace than that? He was utterly approachable to all people especially the downtrodden. All this means that I may not come to church on Sunday, pay my respects to the Pantocrator Christ in the dome, and then go home and do as I please the rest of the week. That same God in the dome became man and identified Himself with every man. "I was hungry and you fed me."

A "Down-to-Earth" Religion

Thus it is that religion "up in the clouds" is immediately brought down to earth. Religion "up in the dome" is immediately brought down to the ground floor of the church, to the person sitting next to me. How I treat my fellow man is how I treat Christ. And how I treat my fellow human is the basis on which I shall be judged by the Pantocrator when I appear before His awesome tribunal.

Centuries ago the Moslems took over a beautiful Orthodox Church in Asia Minor. They immediately plastered over the facade of the Pantocrator in the dome. But as the years went by and the plaster eroded, the face of Christ began to re-appear through the plaster. Try as people may, to remove Christ from life, to cover Him up, to eliminate Him, He remains Pantocrator. Nothing will ever remove Him from the Throne. "The Lord God omnipotent reigns."

A Universe In Chaos

In spite of this there are those for whom God is not Pantocrator, but a powerless God Who has lost control of the universe. H. G. Wells expresses this when he portrays the world as a great stage produced and managed by God. The curtain goes up and all is peaches and cream. The world is ethereally beautiful and the characters are a delight to behold. All is well until the leading man steps on the hem of the dress of the leading lady, who falls over a chair and knocks over a lamp, which overturns a table and brings down the whole back scenery. This brings the whole scenery down in chaos on the heads of the actors. Meanwhile, behind the scenes, God the producer, is frantically running about, pulling strings and shouting orders, trying desperately to restore order, but unable to do so. Orthodox Christianity has never believed in such a powerless and limited God.

God is Pantocrator, limitless, infinite, all-ruling, all-loving, all-caring, holding the reigns of the universe firmly in His hands.

He Is Able

The image of God as Pantocrator conveys the message that God is ABLE, exceedingly able to help in time of need. We express this in the prayer, "Holy God, HOLY MIGHTY, Holy Immortal One, have mercy on us." The Pantocrator, He Who sits on the Throne, is mightily able to help. When the early Christians preached Christ, they preached Him as One Who was alive and strong, able in the power of His resurrection to flood the dark places of the world with light, able to shake the Roman Empire and change the face of history, able to make the weak strong, and the crooked straight.

The word of God tells us that Christ the Pantocrator is:
- ". . . ABLE to do far more than you would ever dare to ask or even dream of" (Eph. 3:20).
- ". . . ABLE to give you everything you need and more" (2 Cor. 9:8).
- ". . . ABLE to save completely all who come to God through Him" (Hebr. 7:25).
- ". . . ABLE to help you when you suffer and are tempted" (Hebr. 2:18).

"... ABLE to keep you from falling away and to bring you sinless and perfect into His glorious presence with shouts of everlasting joy" (Jude 1:24).
"... ABLE to deliver you" (Dan. 3:17).
"... ABLE to safely guard all that you have given Him until the day of His return" (2 Tim. 1:12).
"... ABLE to do anything He promised" (Rom. 4:31).

Is Anything Too Hard For Him?

Someone said once, "When I worry I go to the mirror and say to myself, 'This tremendous thing which is worrying me is beyond a solution. It is especially too hard for my Lord Jesus Christ to handle.' After I have said that, I smile and I am ashamed."

Is anything too hard for the Pantocrator, the One Who rules the universe?

In the words of V. J. Berg,

When we look to man for help,
We get the help of a man.
When we trust society,
We get its tangled plan.
When we depend upon ourselves,
Our impotence shows through.
But when in faith we turn to prayer,
We get what God can do.

Where Is God?

Often a situation arises that causes us grave concern. We become filled with anxiety. We let our imagination paint dark pictures of what might happen. An aching doubt begins to possess us and we begin to wonder whether God is on the Throne. We feel like crying out, "Where is God?"

The cure for such anxious and troubled states of mind is faith, faith that affirms in the midst of danger: "Fear not. God is in charge. He is with me as light and wisdom. He is with me as healing power. He is with me as my source of supply. He is with me as love and forgiveness. He is in charge — still on the Throne. I find peace and strength in this assurance."

For we believe in a God Who chose not to remain on His Throne, but took on our form and became one with us. He knows our needs, our pain, our fears, because He came to live with us. He reigns on the Throne but with a compassion for us that is beyond expression.

The Connection That Makes The Difference

Someone said to a reformed alcoholic, "I see you have overcome the mastery of the devil at last." "No," came the quiet answer, "but I do have the Master of the devil—the Pantocrator Christ within me."

In order to receive power from the All-Powerful Pantocrator, we must get attached and stay attached to Him through faith, prayer and the sacraments. As the branch that remains attached to the vine receives nourishment and life, so the one who maintains a living connection with Jesus through prayer, receives power to live, power to overcome. Like the railway tickets we used to see that said, "Not good if detached," we are not good, we are weak, powerless, ineffective, if we are detached from the Pantocrator.

We have to be connected. We were created to be connected. For Jesus, the place where everything connected was prayer. It was where God and man came together in a glorious union. "I and the Father are one," He said. Connected! "You will be one with us too," He said to the disciples, "if you pray; if you abide in us." Prayer is where everything gets connected. Being connected with the Pantocrator Christ puts me in touch with infinite power and opens the way to unbounded possibilities.

For, Jesus is not just a great Example; He is also the Great Enabler, the All-Powerful Pantocrator with Whom I can connect.

Ever-Present

The icon of the Pantocrator in the dome should remind us that God's Presence hovers just above us not only when we are in church but wherever we may be. He is there as we sleep at night. He is there when we work during the day. He is there when we relax. He is there when we are being tempted. He is there when we are bedridden with illness. He will be there when the final moment of life comes. In fact, our faith should help us visualize the Pantocrator Christ hovering above us constantly as we go through life. Finally, one day those everlasting arms will reach down to lift us and carry us into the fullness of His presence, into the bright side of His love.

"All Is Well, I Have Seen His Face"

A person was greatly worried about a terrible storm at sea. It was his first ocean trip and he had never seen such huge waves. But as lightning flashed he caught sight of the captain on the bridge and there was a smile on his face. That was all he needed. He now felt secure. And he began to encourage the other fearful passengers huddled below deck by telling them, "I have seen the face of the captain and he smiled. All is well."

That is what looking at the serene face of the Pantocrator should do to us: restore calm, buttress us from within, and give us strength for the journey of life. "If God is for us, who is against us? He Who did not spare His own Son but gave Him up for us all, will He not also give us all things with Him?" (Rom. 8:31-32)

A Captain at the Controls

I have been in the cockpit of a jumbo jet. There are so many controls that one wonders how anyone can know what they are all for. But the captain knows and using them, he lifts that huge aircraft off the ground with the greatest ease. Is it only a jumbo jet that needs a captain? Is there no Captain guiding the cosmos? Is there no Pantocrator at the controls? One Who knows exactly when and how to push all the proper switches and buttons to control the universe He created? People who don't believe this, lose life's meaning and joy. Imagine how desolate it must feel to believe that you are on a planet hurtling through space with no one at the controls!

Fall Down Before Him

There is a very touching story told of Queen Victoria. Handel's "Messiah" was first played in England in the Queen's honor. It was the custom for people to rise to their feet at the "Hallelujah Chorus," but everyone felt the Queen should remain seated by reason of her station. Yet when the great strains of majestic music floated out, "And He shall reign for ever and ever. He shall reign for ever and ever," the Queen rose to her feet. She lifted the crown from her head and stood with bowed head with the rest of the people.

"And He shall reign forever and ever." The Lord God omnipotent—the Pantocrator—reigns! But the question is, "Does He reign as King and Pantocrator on the throne of your heart and mine?" If He does, then like the twenty-four elders in Chapter 4 of the Book of Revelation, let us "fall down before Him Who is seated on the throne and worship Him Who lives for ever and ever." Like them, let us take off the crowns of our pride and cast them before His Throne as we sing,

"Worthy art Thou, our Lord and God,
to receive glory and honor and power,
for Thou didst create all things,
and by Thy will they existed and were created."
Alleluia. Alleluia. Alleluia.

Chapter **11**

The Divine Liturgy: Reality Not Symbol

A couple was leaving church after Sunday services. "Did you see that designer suit on the woman in front of us?" the wife asked. "And the hat on that woman across the aisle? And the frilly blue dress on the woman sitting to your left?"

"Well, no," the husband was quick to confess. "I'm afraid I dozed off." She gave him a sharp look. "A lot of good church does you!"

In "The Screwtape Letters" C. S. Lewis shows how temptation comes anywhere, anytime, but especially when we are at prayer or worship. Screwtape was one of hell's under-secretaries who had agents on earth. He would write letters to his agents, informing them how they should keep their charges from worshipping God. One day an angel wrote telling him that his charge had joined a church, and wondering how he should handle the situation. Screwtape wrote back to his agent suggesting that he never leave him, that he go with him to church. There he was to try by all means to distract his charge from true worship by whispering to him that the usher is a hypocrite, by getting him to concentrate on what people are wearing, by daydreaming, by thinking of possible business deals, etc. "Above all," said Screwtape, "never let him see the Church with all its banners flying. For at that sight all of hell trembles."

Ignorance A Distraction

I submit that another way the devil uses to distract us from true worship is ignorance. Coming to the liturgy we see a lot of processions, vestments, icons. We hear Byzantine hymnology. We smell incense. We are told to sit, stand, cross ourselves. All of this is good. The Orthodox liturgy, we are told, captures and expresses the mystery of God. But if we are ignorant of what is going on in the liturgy, the whole thing, including God, will remain a great mystery to us. The devil will actually be coming to church with us and using our ignorance, among many other means, to prevent us from truly worshipping God.

The Arena of Renewal

The liturgy is a great source of renewal since it brings to us today the Christ Who alone makes all things new. The meaning of the breaking of the bread and the offering of the cup in the liturgy lies in the fact that the very life of God Himself flows into us. The life that streams forth from the source of the life-giving Trinity comes to abide in us. In Christ we are renewed. We pass from slavery to freedom, from darkness to light, from death to life. The arena where this renewal happens is the liturgy and the sacraments.

The Centrality of The Liturgy

It is no wonder, then, that the liturgy occupies such a central place in Orthodox worship.

A Russian Orthodox priest said to a visitor in Moscow in 1976, "Our sufferings have brought us back to the essentials. Now, as never before, we understand that the Church exists in and for the Eucharist. So much else has been taken away from us, but the celebration of the liturgy remains; and in this one thing we have everything."

When the envoys of Prince Vladimir arrived in Constaninople to inquire about the Christian faith, they were not offered a verbal explanation. Rather, they were taken to the Church of the Holy Wisdom to witness the celebration of the liturgy. It was the action of the Liturgy that converted them.

The other sacraments, such as baptism and marriage, were originally performed in conjunction with the celebration of the Liturgy. In the Orthodox Marriage Service today, the couple drink from a cup of wine. In earlier times, the cup was actually the chalice. They both received Communion. They partook of the Eucharist which truly united them, making them one in Christ. The Liturgy has been the source and font of the other sacraments.

Professor Ion Bria writes, "It has rightly been said that the best way of access to the heart of the Orthodox Church is the 'divine liturgy,' the celebration of the holy mysteries (Eucharist). If people would like to know what Orthodox Christians believe in, whom they worship, and how they live, they should penetrate the form and substance of the liturgy."[49]

Nicholas Kabasilas calls the liturgy the final and greatest of the mysteries, "since it is not possible to go beyond it or add anything to it. After the liturgy there is nowhere to go. There all must stand, and try to examine the means by which we may preserve the treasure to the end. For in it we obtain God Himself, and God is united with us in the most perfect union" (The Life of Christ 4. 1,3).

Speaking on the centrality of the liturgy, Fr. John Meyendorff writes:

> *"Byzantine Christianity is known for the wealth of its liturgy, a wealth which reflects indeed a theological . . . position. Through the liturgy a Byzantine recognized and experienced his membership in the Body of Christ. While a Western Christian generally checked his faith against external authority (the magisterium or the Bible), the Byzantine Christian considered the liturgy both a source and an expression of his theology . . ."*[50]

The centrality of the liturgy in the Orthodox Church is helping it survive one of the greatest persecutions in history. Speaking of a visit to the Soviet Union, Lesslie Newbigin wrote:

> *"Some years ago I had the privilege of sharing in the worship of one of the great churches in Moscow. It was an unforgettable experience. The Russian Church has lived for more than half a century under extreme pressure. One of the most powerful governments in the*

> *world has deliberately sought to destroy it. Every kind of outward activity in teaching, preaching or service has been forbidden. The one corporate activity which is left to the Church is its worship. Into that worship the faithful of Russia throw everything they have. Because of that worship the Russian Church is still a reality, continuing to draw men and women to faith in God, even in the midst of an aggressively atheistic culture . . ."*[51]

It is no wonder that, when asked what the Orthodox Church is, Patriarch Alexei of Moscow said, "It is the Church that celebrates the divine liturgy."

Fr. John of Kronstadt

Speaking on the centrality of the liturgy in Orthodox worship, Fr. John of Kronstadt wrote:

> *"The divine liturgy is truly a heavenly service on earth, in which God Himself, in a particular, immediate and most close manner is present and dwells with men, for He Himself is the invisible celebrant of the service; He is both the offerer and the offering. There is on earth nothing higher, greater, more holy, than the liturgy; nothing more solemn, nothing more life-giving.*
>
> *Great is the liturgy. In it there is recalled the life, not of some great man, but of God incarnate, who suffered and died for us, who rose again and ascended into heaven, and who shall come again to judge the whole world.*
>
> *The liturgy is the continually repeated enactment of God's love to mankind, and of His all-powerful mediation for the salvation of the whole world, and of every member of the human race separately. It is the marriage of the lamb, the marriage of the King's Son, in which the bride of the Son of God is every faithful soul, and the giver of the bride the Holy Ghost.*
>
> *The liturgy is the supper, the table of God's love to mankind. Around the Lamb of God on the paten all*

are at this time assembled—the living and the dead, the holy and the sinful, the Church above and the Church below.

God has opened for us, in His Body and Blood, the source of living water, flowing into life eternal, and gives himself to be our food and drink, that we might live through Him." [52]

What Is The Liturgy?

Let us consider now what the liturgy is.

Fr. Schmemann said, "The liturgy is, first of all, the Paschal gathering of those who are to meet the Risen Lord and enter with Him into His kingdom."

Nicholas Gogol wrote, "The liturgy is the eternal repetition of the great act of love for us."

The central event of the liturgy is the descent, the appearance, and the divine presence of the resurrected Christ. A person is frequently reminded of this presence. For example, at one point in the liturgy the priest says, "Christ is in our midst." The co-celebrant priest responds, after exchanging the kiss of peace, "He is and will ever be."

Paul Evdokimov wrote, "During the liturgy, through its divine power, we are projected to the point where eternity cuts across time, and at this point we become true contemporaries with the events we commemorate."

The Eucharist is the Biblical wedding supper at which the celestial Bridegroom—Jesus—weds the pure bride, the chosen congregation, you and me. It is the consummation of the love relationship between God and man.

The liturgy is the place where one can "lay aside all worldly care," as the Cherubic Hymn invites us, "to receive the King of all."

The liturgy is where the saving deeds of Christ are made present to us today so that we may participate in them. Christ becomes our contemporary; Christ Who is "the same yesterday, today and forever."

To participate in the liturgy is to experience the kingdom of God. This is aptly expressed by the Trisagion which is the hymn of the Seraphim as they eternally glorify the Trinity before the heavenly throne. "Man is, as it were, transported into heaven itself," writes St. John Chrysostom. "He stands near the throne of glory. He flies with the Seraphim. He sings the most holy hymn" (XLVIII, 734c). In the words of Jean Danielou, "We are no longer on earth but . . . in heaven. Restored by Baptism to the angelic creation from which he fell by sin, the newly-baptized once more can unite his voice with that of the angels. He is admitted to the official worship of creation, of which the angels are representatives. And at the center of this worship is the priestly action of Christ in His Passion and Resurrection."

St. Gregory Palamas writes that through the liturgy "by this flesh (of Christ in the Eucharist) our community is raised to heaven; that is where this Bread truly dwells; and we enter into the Holy of Holies by the pure offering of the Body of Christ" (Homily 56).

Fr. Alkiviadis Calivas defines the liturgy as follows, "The Divine Liturgy celebrates the inrush of eternal life into our perishable, mortal existence and the abolition of our deaths. . . . The future life is infused into the present one and blended with it, so that 'our fallen humanity may be transformed into the glorified humanity of the new Adam, Christ.' . . . Each Divine Liturgy is a continuation of the mystery of Pentecost. It is the renewal and the confirmation of the coming of the Holy Spirit Who is ever present in the Church" (*The Greek Orthodox Theological Review,* Winter, 1984).

The liturgy has also been defined as the sacrament of Christ's permanent saving presence among us in the age of the Church.

Non-Orthodox liturgical scholars tell us that the Orthodox Church has preserved the liturgical spirit of the early Church and continues to live by it and to draw life from its source.[53]

Because the East looks upon the Church as "heaven on earth," a view that the Greek Fathers loved to stress, the liturgy became an icon of the celestial liturgy described in the Epistle to the Hebrews and the Apocalypse. In the words of Fr. Robert Taft, "The Westerner sees the liturgy as a means of preparing the militant Christian 'to fight the good fight.' . . . The Easterner looks to the liturgical community's transfiguring participation in the eternally triumphant God-man's Passover from death to life." The Gothic Cathedrals of the West were built to resemble fortresses to which the Christian flees for protection and strength. The Eastern cathedrals, like Sancta Sophia, were built to resemble palaces where one comes to experience the kingdom of God on earth.

I'm not saying one is better than the other; I think we need both. Both the fortress and the palace concepts are valid expressions of what the church of Jesus should be for us.

The liturgy is THEOPHANY, the manifestation or appearance of God. The icon screen with the opening of the Royal Gates witness to this. The Royal Gates are opened and the presence of God is revealed in the word of God (the Gospel Book) which sits enthroned upon the holy table and in the tabernacle which contains the Presanctified Gifts: Jesus the Lamb of God and the Bread of Life.

Fr. Robert Taft has written, "The purpose of God's saving revelation is to render man capable of the life of God, and the liturgy is the privileged ground of this encounter. It is the place of theophany, where man is introduced into the divine life by participating in the mystery of redemption."

In the Orthodox Church the doctrine of the atonement is a liturgical doctrine. What our Savior did for us on Calvary and at the tomb is not left in the distant past. It is made present again in the Liturgy (Eucharist) and the Sacraments.

In the first part of the liturgy, the liturgy of the word, Christ comes to us as the LOGOS, the Word of God. In the second part of the liturgy, the liturgy of the faithful, He comes to us as the LAMB OF GOD Who takes away the sins of the world. He comes to us in every liturgy as both the Word and Lamb of God, speaking to us and uniting Himself with us.

It is unfortunate that through the centuries for may reasons preaching and the people's communion were gradually and largely divorced from the liturgy. Both have always been an integral part of the Orthodox liturgy and we are pleased to see that a form of liturgical revival is now occurring in some of our churches. Both the preaching of God's word and the people's communion are being restored to their proper place in the liturgy.

The liturgy is Pentecost as well as Easter. The epiclesis prayer is an invocation to the Holy Spirit that He come upon us first, and then upon the gifts of bread and wine to change them into the Body and Blood of our Savior. Listen to the words of the epiclesis:

"We offer unto Thee this spiritual and bloodless service; and we pray, we beseech and implore Thee:

Send down Thy Holy Spirit upon us and upon these gifts here set forth."

The liturgy is more even than Easter and Pentecost. It is a calling to remembrance and making present again of all the sacred events in the history of our salvation. As the prayer of the liturgy says:

"Remembering therefore . . . all those things which came to pass for our sakes; the cross, the tomb, the resurrection on the third day, the ascension into heaven, the sitting on the right hand, the coming again a second time in glory."

In the liturgy, by sharing the Body and Blood of Jesus, we become partakers of divine nature (2 Peter 1:4) and experience a foretaste of the kingdom, which was inaugurated at the incarnation in Bethlehem and manifested at Pentecost in the Upper Room.

___ A Personal Encounter With the Living Christ ___

The Divine Liturgy is not simply a sacred drama, a mere representation of past events, or a symbolic depiction of the life of Jesus. More than anything else, it is a personal encounter with the living, resurrected Christ. It is the place where the Christian meets Christ in the fullness of His redeeming activity, the place where Christ is made present, or better still, makes Himself present. This personal encounter with Christ effected through the Holy Spirit in the liturgy is beautifully expressed in the private pre-communion prayers where the soul enters into a lovely personal dialogue with the Master expressing unworthiness, penitence as well as joy at the coming union. The *Nunc Dimittis* or *Nyn Apolyis* of St. Symeon, repeated by our Church at every Vesper service, and by the priest to himself at the end of every liturgy, serves to reassure us that in every liturgy, we see the Savior Jesus with the eyes of our soul, as Symeon saw Him with his physical eyes; we speak to Him; He speaks to us; we receive Him not into our arms but into our soul through the Eucharist, and we leave filled with peace and joy.

"Lord, now lettest thou thy servant
  depart in peace,
 according to thy word;
 for mine eyes have seen thy salvation

which thou hast prepared in the presence of all peoples, a light for revelation to the Gentiles, and for glory of thy people Israel'' (Luke 2:29-32).

St. Maximus the Confessor has written:

The grace of the Holy Spirit, which is always invisibly present, [is present] in a distinctly special way during the hours of the holy liturgy; each person who is found present there, grace transforms, remolds, and truly remodels into a more divine image, conformed to the Spirit Himself; it guides him into the meaning of the mysteries celebrated, even if he himself may not notice it (Chapter 24).

―――――――――――――― *Pervading Joy* ――――――――――――――

A spirit of joy pervades the liturgy. Peter Hammond wrote, "Her liturgy (the Orthodox Church) still enshrines that element of sheer joy in the Resurrection of the Lord that we find in so many of the early Christian writings."

Professor Edmund Schlink, a Lutheran theologian, describes the joy that pervades the Orthodox liturgy as follows:

"In praising Christ's victory on the cross and in the resurrection and in the adoration of the Holy Trinity, the glory that is to come is experienced as a present reality. The worshippers are translated into that glory, and the menace of the material world grows dim. In no other church does the liturgy so triumphantly unfold the victory of Christ with its implications for the whole cosmos, or laud or magnify in such a rapturous way the presence of the New Creation that is to come. The liturgy of the Eastern Church resounds with the eschatological exultation with which the early Christians celebrated the Lord's Supper."

Fr. Alexander Schmemann also describes the liturgy in terms of joy:

"The Eucharist is the entrance of the Church into the joy of its Lord. And to enter into that joy, so as to be a witness to it in the world, is indeed the very

> *calling of the Church, its essential* leitourgia, *the sacrament by which it 'becomes what it is . . .' The liturgy is, before everything else, the joyous gathering of those who are to meet the risen Lord and to enter with Him into the bridal chamber. And it is this joy of expectation and this expectation of joy that are expressed in singing and ritual, in vestments and in censing, in that whole 'beauty' of the liturgy, which has so often been denounced as unnecessary and even sinful."* [54]

Two Other Liturgies

One of the purposes of the liturgy is to activate an inner liturgy in the mind and heart of the worshipper where God will be kept in constant remembrance so that prayers and intercessions may be offered to Him ceaselessly. As the heart, for example, prays the Jesus Prayer, the "inner liturgy" is being celebrated in the chapel of the soul. The Church Fathers speak of a *krupti ergasia* "a secret work," going on constantly in the mind and heart of the true believer. By this they mean that the mind and heart were constantly tuned to God, praying psalms and practicing His presence even while the outer person was engaged in manual labor. The Divine Liturgy serves to initiate and foster the inner liturgy that takes place in the mind and heart of the believer.

An example of the inner liturgy celebrated in the mind and heart of the believer is provided by Anatoli Levitin who was in a Soviet prison for carrying out an informal religious program for young people. He tells how he celebrated the liturgy in his heart each day:

> *The greatest miracle of all is prayer. I have only to turn my thoughts to God and I suddenly feel a force bursting into me; there is new strength in my soul, in my entire being. . . . The basis of my whole spiritual life is the Orthodox liturgy, so while I was in prison I attended it every day in my imagination. At 8:00 in the morning I would begin walking around my cell, repeating its words to myself. I was then inseparably linked to the whole Christian world. In the Great Litany I would always pray for the Pope and for the*

> *Ecumenical Patriarch, as well as for the leaders of my own church. At the central point of the liturgy . . . I felt myself standing before the face of the Lord, sensing almost physically his wounded, bleeding body. I would begin praying in my own words, remembering all those near to me, those in prison and those who were free, those still alive and those who had died. More and more names welled up from my memory. . . . The prison walls moved apart and the whole universe became my residence, visible and invisible, the universe for which that wounded, pierced body offered itself as a sacrifice. . . . After this, I experienced an exaltation of spirit all day—I felt purified within. Not only my own prayer helped me, but even more the prayer of many other faithful Christians. I felt it continually, working from a distance, lifting me up as though on wings, giving me living water and the bread of life, peace of soul, rest and love.*[55]

In addition to the inner liturgy of the heart, the Divine Liturgy leads to the so-called liturgy after the liturgy. This is the liturgy of *diakonia* and *martyria* that is celebrated in the world after we leave church. The liturgy feeds our action in the world. It becomes the font of our energy enabling us to become other Christs in the world. Jesus prayed, "As Thou didst send me into the world, so I have sent them into the world" (John 17:18). Thus, we see that there are really not one but three liturgies: the one celebrated at the holy table; the inner liturgy where the heart prays to God especially in the chapel of the soul; and thirdly the liturgy we celebrate in the world.

Erasmus said once, "I think there are far too many who count up how many times they attend the liturgy and rely almost entirely upon this for their salvation. They are convinced that they owe nothing further to Christ. Leaving church they immediately return to their former habits. I certainly do not hesitate to praise them for getting to the liturgy, but I am forced to condemn them for stopping at this point."

The liturgy continues when we leave church. After the dismissal the congregation moves out the church door into the world to be apostles for Christ, to continue the liturgy of martyria (witness) and diakonia (service).

The ancient form of the liturgy concluded with the words "Let us go forth in peace." We see clearly in these words of dismissal that the liturgy concludes with mission. These words are not an ending but a beginning. They invite us to mission and service in the world. As Jesus commanded us to *GO* INTO ALL THE WORLD TO PREACH AND BAPTIZE, so the liturgy concludes with the call for us to go back into the world as apostles (ones who are sent) with a mission. Thus, the liturgy shows us that the Eucharist is the beginning, the alpha point, of a cosmic transfiguration. It nourishes, feeds and sustains us as we fight against poverty, disease, and injustice. The liturgy concludes with a call for us to go out into the world and build up the kingdom. In peace, *go*—we are told—and begin the "liturgy after the liturgy."

I once asked during the children's sermon, "What do you like about church?" One little boy replied honestly, "Leaving." Though I hadn't expected that response, the boy started me thinking. In a way, leaving could really be the highlight of each liturgy. At the end of the liturgy the church is sent into the world, to serve, to love, to minister. What if we opened the church doors and a bunch of ready-and-willing-to-serve, chomping-at-the-bit Christians rushed out joyfully to proclaim the gospel and to love those around them to Christ? Leaving really is the best part of the liturgy—not leaving to go home and watch television and lie around, but leaving to go out and to enlighten, enliven, involve, encourage, uplift and love in the name of Christ.

I like what Fr. Calivas says, "Sharing in the life of Christ and energized by the gifts of the Holy Spirit, the Church becomes *an epiphany of love."* Nowhere can this be more evident than in "the liturgy after the liturgy" when we are sent out into the world to look for the suffering Christ in people, especially the poor, the sick, the unbelieving, etc. The Church may not be *of* the world but she is very much *in* the world and *for* the world. Did not Jesus give Himself "for the life of the world" (John 6:51)?

A priest told of a little deaf and dumb girl to whom he had tried to be especially kind. Using sign language she asked him, "Are you so nice to me because you really love me, or because you are supposed to be nice?" If the Church is the epiphany of God's love in Christ, then it needs to speak in the only language the world understands: love—the love we receive in sharing the life of Christ.

A priest tells of a family whose house was destroyed by fire. They had no insurance. That Sunday he said to his people from the pulpit: "True worship is giving ourselves to God fully, offering ourselves as a living sacrifice. I want us all to go home and round up food, clothing, blankets, and money and meet back here in an hour. We'll take the liturgy to our friends." An hour later they piled into the little house, each carrying food and clothing. The church presented a check. Someone in the congregation loaned a trailer. They took the liturgy to this needy family. They, in effect, celebrated "the liturgy after the liturgy." The real liturgy of love and service in Christ's name begins when we leave church.

Liturgical Living

The word *leitourgia* is derived from the two Greek words *laos* (people, especially the people of God) and *ergon* (act). Thus, a very proper translation of liturgy would be "the people of God performing God's work." When the divine liturgy is concluded in church, I "depart in peace" to do God's work in the world, to live liturgically. In liturgical living as in liturgical worship, we yield ourselves to Christ to be used by Him as His instruments in the world today. Truly, He has no hands but ours to do His work in the world today. As Mother Teresa says, "In the liturgy we have Jesus in the appearance of bread, while in the slums we see Christ and touch Him in the broken bodies, in the abandoned children." The broken bread that we receive in the liturgy must be transformed into a bread we break for the millions of starving. As Fr. Walter Burghardt so well says, "If I am to be a eucharist for the life of the world, my feeding on the flesh of Christ must take me from church to world, to wash the feet of my brothers and sisters." The "real presence" of Christ in the Eucharist must become in me a real presence to those about me who hunger for food or freedom, for peace or truth, or for a better understanding of God. As the epiclesis prayer says, "We offer unto Thee this reasonable worship, for the whole world." It is for the needs of the whole world that we are sent out to perform each week "the liturgy after the liturgy," offering hospitality to strangers, care for the distressed, liberation for the oppressed, healing for the sick, and compassion for all, enduring death daily (2 Cor. 11:23-24).

Taking Jesus Into the World

A certain church had burned to the ground. Only a statue of Jesus was salvaged. It was placed by the firemen on the sidewalk in front of the church. An unchurched neighbor observed the statue and said, "This is the first time that those people have ever taken Jesus out of that church." May that be never said of us! One of our main tasks in "the liturgy after the liturgy" is to take Jesus out of church and into the world.

Dead Sea Souls

The Dead Sea is dead because it has no exit, no overflow. The Jordan River flows into it but not through it. It just stays there and becomes stagnant. There are also Dead Sea souls today. They come to the liturgy, receive the many blessings of the Holy Trinity, but keep them locked up in themselves. They do not share with others the blessings they receive. Their faith has no exit. It was never intended to be that way. The liturgy is not finished in church. It begins in church and is completed in the world. "When does the liturgy begin?" someone phoned to ask. The pastor replied, "It begins when we leave church." We not only go to the liturgy, we are the liturgy wherever we go. We become the real presence of Christ in the world. In the words of the Apostle James,

"If anyone thinks that he is a worshipper of God, and yet does not bridle his tongue, his worship is an empty thing. This is pure and undefiled worship, as God the Father sees it, to visit the orphans and the widows, and to keep oneself unspotted from the world" (James 1:26-27).

Ascension Leads to Mission

Fr. Alexander Schmemann put it this way, "This is the meaning of the Eucharist; this is why the mission of the Church begins in the liturgy of ascension, for it alone makes possible the liturgy of mission."[56] We ascend to the throne of God in the liturgy that we may descend to minister to God's people in the valley of this world. If the Orthodox Church prides itself on its liturgy, it must never forget that the liturgy that begins at the holy table does not end there. It is consummated in the world through our ministry of *diakonia* (service) and *martyria* (witness).

The Huddle

The liturgy is much like the huddle in a football game. The players gather in a circle before each play, and the quarterback gives them the next play, making sure each player knows his assignment. But the huddle is not the game. The game is played when the players line up in their positions on the field and carry out their assignments. The liturgy is much like a huddle. It prepares us for our service, "for the life of the world." As one communist visitor to the U.S.A. said when he saw hundreds of people leaving church after liturgy one Sunday, "What do they do now?" The answer is that they now go out to perform another liturgy, a liturgy which, if performed well, would eliminate the glaring inequities and injustices which gave birth to Communism.

The Criticism of Other Worldliness

The Orthodox Church has been criticized as being too otherworldly. Its liturgy is magnificently beautiful and inspiring but unfortunately it has often locked Jesus in the liturgy. It is so easy to forget that the liturgy continues when we leave church. How much we need to be reminded of the magnificent prayers in the liturgy of St. Basil wherein he remembers and prays for almost every need in the world:

> *"Nourish the infants; instruct the young, succour the aged; comfort the faint-hearted; gather together into one them that are scattered, bring them back which went astray and unite them in Thy Holy . . . Church. Set free them that are vexed with unclean spirits. Sail with them that sail; journey with them that journey. Defend the widows; shelter the orphans; deliver the captives; help the sick.*
>
> *Remember, O God, them that stand trial, that are in prisons, that live in exile; and all that are in affliction and tribulation . . ."*

Our Job Description For the Liturgy in the World

This magnificent prayer in the liturgy of St. Basil establishes a job description for what we are called to do in "the liturgy after the liturgy." Certainly the liturgy does not end with just a prayer for the infants, the young, the aged, the faint-hearted, the scattered, the widows, the sick, the imprisoned, and the exiled. It proceeds from prayer to practice. Otherwise, we are like those condemned by the Apostle James: "What does it profit, my brethren, if a man says he has faith, but has not works? Can his faith save him? If a brother or sister is ill-clad and in lack of daily food, and one of you says to them, 'Go in peace, be warmed and filled,' without giving them the things needed for the body, what does it profit? So faith by itself, if it has no works, is dead" (James 2:14-17).

Thus, the Divine Liturgy, far from ending when we leave church, actually gives birth to two other liturgies that we celebrate after we leave church, i.e., the inner liturgy of prayer and praise offered ceaselessly in the chapel of the soul, and the liturgy of service and witness that we celebrate in the world for the orphans, the aged, the sick, the widows, the imprisoned and the starving. Would you call this "otherworldly?"

A Brief Walk Through the Liturgy

Have you ever wondered why there is repetition in the liturgy? For example, how many times is the petition "Again and again let us pray to the Lord" repeated, calling on us to pray the same petitions all over again? Many may be irritated by this repetition or consider it superflous and time-consuming. Yet listen to how Tito Colliander, the great Finnish literary figure, explains the need for such repetition in the liturgy:

"But how often does it happen that the birds of inattentiveness which are spoken of in the Parable of the Sower and which are sent by the Devil come and carry away the seeds which have just been sown. We have neglected to follow with our hearts the words of the prayers as they were pronounced by the priest; we had ears but we did not hear. In that case, he who is praying in church has a chance to be more attentive the next time the same prayer is repeated during the service. And then he feels the immense warmth of thanksgiving. In this way our Church has taken care of us weaklings and given us the opportunity again and again to enter into prayer's life-creating com-

munion with the Lord and to practice perseverance in prayer, just as the athlete trains himself in running and throwing. Or to be watered over and over again, just as a plant growing in arid soil is watered in order to take root.''

The Little Entrance Not Symbolic

Many believe that the little entrance of the liturgy when the priest carries the Gospel book in procession out to the people is a beautiful symbolic ceremony. It symbolizes the beginning of Christ's preaching ministry at age thirty. But this procession is anything but symbolic. It is real. Christ actually comes today to address us personally with His words of everlasting life. It is a real personal encounter with the Lord of life. To listen to His words as spoken through the Gospel lesson is to gain life; to fail to listen is to choose death.

Thus, as the multitudes went to hear Jesus on the Mount of Beatitudes; as they flocked to Him to be fed the five loaves and two fish; as the dying thief on the cross implored Him for mercy, and as the disciples sat with Him at the Last Supper, so we may approach Jesus today through the liturgy. In fact, in the early Church the small entrance marked the entrance of the clergy and the people into the Church to be with Jesus Who comes to us as He came to the multitudes of His day: to teach us His word, to feed us the Bread of Life, to forgive us as He forgave the penitent thief, to give us His Body and Blood as He did to His disciples at the Last Supper. All this is not symbolic but real. In this case, to concentrate on symbolism is to miss the reality of Christ's presence in our midst here and now.

The Great Entrance: Our Ascension to God

In like manner the Great Entrance of the liturgy when our gifts of bread and wine, representing us, are carried in procession into the altar and laid on the holy table, is not symbolic. It is a real entrance—our entrance to the throne of God. For in Christ we have been given access to heaven. We are united to God and made participants of Christ's entrance into the kingdom. When the Church sings the hymn which the angels sing eternally before the throne of God: ''Holy, holy, holy, is the Lord of Sabaoth . . .''

and when the priest prays, "Holy God, Who art praised with the thrice holy voice of the Seraphim, glorified by the Cherubim and adored by all the hosts of heaven . . ." the angels, as Fr. Schmemann so well said, are not "for decoration and inspiration." They are not symbolic. They are really there and we are really in heaven. The liturgy is our real entrance, passage, ascension to heaven, to the throne of God. To use again the words of Fr. Schmemann, *"Holy* is the word, the song, the 'reaction' of the Church as it enters into heaven, as it stands before the heavenly glory of God."

Fr. Stanley Harakas calls our attention to the danger of symbolization in the Liturgy:

> *"Liturgiologists almost unanimously criticize the tendency which developed in late Byzantium to give—'mystical interpretations'—to everything conceivable connected with the conduct of the Liturgy. Thus, the decorative tassels on the priestly stole were interpreted to mean the souls of the faithful which were dependent upon the priest's ministrations! The historians of the Liturgy pointed out that such—'symbolization'—served to distract attention from the true meaning of the Liturgy as a sacramental action uniting the believer with Christ and manifesting the Church as a reality in the world. However, there was another consequence which was equally serious. It created an attitude in the attendees which might be appropriately characterized as that of the—'tourist-observer'—. . .*
>
> *It is a 'this-means-that' approach which places the worshipper in the position of an outsider who receives a tourist's description of the event. At most, he or she can—upon a return to the site—remember what means what. Remarkably, this is also true of the approach of the historical liturgiologist. If he explains the historical origins of the Great Entrance and connects it with ancient Byzantine imperial practices, for example, the worshipper is still a—'tourist-observer.' Barring a radical rewriting and revision of the text of the Divine Liturgy (a highly unlikely event in the*

Eastern Orthodox Church), the generally accepted and taught symbolisms can be retained, but they must be approached in a devotional manner which emphasizes the conscious and heart-felt participation of the Christian worshipper. . . . The Divine Liturgy seems to call for that kind of participatory involvement in its symbolism." [57]

The late Fr. Alexander Schmemann warned us against the symbolization of the liturgy: "In my own tradition, the Byzantine, this has meant the appearance of endless symbolic explanations of worship, and so the eucharistic Liturgy that is at the heart of the Church has been transformed in effect into a series of audio-visual aids. Symbolism is discerned everywhere. I tried once to collect all the meanings of the exclamation before the Creed, 'The doors! The doors!,' and I found about sixteen different and mutually exclusive explanations. Or else the seven episcopal vestments were identified with the seven gifts of the Holy Spirit. It is not that I deny episcopacy as a source of grace. But certainly those seven items of vesture were not originally intended to illustrate that. . . . If we are to recover the real meaning of the liturgy, we need to go back, behind the commentaries with their symbolic explanations, to the actual text and celebration of the Eucharist itself. We are to see in the Liturgy the fulfillment of the Church at the table of the Lord in the kingdom." [58]

——————— *A Journey to The Kingdom* ———————

The liturgy begins with a doxology that announces its destination: "Blessed is the kingdom of the Father and of the Son and of the Holy Spirit now and forevermore." The liturgy is a journey that will take us to the kingdom of God not symbolically but in reality, as Fr. Schmemann has emphasized. As a bus driver announces at the beginning where the bus is going, so the priest announces at the very beginning that the goal of the liturgy is to take us to the kingdom of God. We hear this and we reply by saying, "Amen." This means, "O.K. This is where we want to go." The word "Amen," writes Fr. Schmemann, "is indeed one of the most important words in the world, for it expresses the agreement of the Church to follow Christ in His ascension to His Father, to make this ascension the destiny of man. . . . Upon this

Amen the fate of the human race is decided. It reveals that the movement toward God has begun."[59]

Doxology

The dominant theme of our Orthodox Christian faith is doxology and praise. Most often the liturgy in the Orthodox Church is preceded by the singing of the great Doxology which sets the tone for the entire liturgy which is one of complete *efcharistia:* gratitude and praise. "Glory be to the Father and to the Son and to the Holy Spirit . . ." "Blessed be the kingdom of God the Father . . . Son . . . and Holy Spirit." This is the major theme of Orthodox worship as it was the dominant motif of the early Christians. What do we find in the New Testament? Tribulation, demons, suffering, crucifixion—yet always with a doxology because Christ has taken the worst of man and overcome it. "In the world you have tribulation, but be of good cheer I have overcome the world." said Jesus. Not crucifixion but resurrection has the last word! Not death but life! Is it any wonder that thanksgiving and praise and doxology are not only the dominant theme but also the whole life style of the Christian?

The liturgy never ceases to glorify and thank God for all He has done and is doing for our salvation as we see in this beautiful prayer of the liturgy: "Thou didst bring us from non-being into being; and didst raise us up that were fallen away; and left nothing undone till Thou hadst lifted us to heaven, and hadst bestowed upon us the kingdom to come. For all these things we give thanks unto Thee . . . for all whereof we know and whereof we know not; for benefits both manifest and hid which Thou hadst wrought upon us . . ."

Prayer and Faith

One of the principles of Orthodox theology is expressed in the Latin saying, "Lex orandi est lex credendi" which means, "How we pray reflects how we believe." The theology of the Church is to be found in the hymns of the Church. The hymns of the liturgy accomplish this in a superb manner. For example, only a very obtuse worshipper can sing aloud the famous O MONOGENIS hymn every Sunday and lack a sense of what we believe as Orthodox Christians:

> *"O only begotten Son and Word of God, though You are immortal You condescended for our salvation to take flesh from the holy Mother of God and ever-virgin Mary and, without undergoing change, You became man. You were crucified, Christ our God, by Your death trampling upon death. You Who are one of the Holy Trinity and are glorified with the Father and the Holy Spirit, save us!"*

Who can sing the Cherubic hymn Sunday after Sunday and not know that he is in the presence of God's glory:

> *"Let us who mystically represent the Cherubim and sing the thrice-holy hymn to the life-giving Trinity now put aside all earthly care, so that we may welcome the King of all who comes escorted by invisible hosts of angels. Alleluia. Alleluia. Alleluia."*

Or who can sing the following Cherubic hymn on Holy Saturday and not know that he is present before the King of Kings:

> *"Let all mortal flesh keep silence and in fear and trembling stand, pondering nothing earthly-minded. For the King of Kings and the Lord of Lords cometh forth to the faithful. Before Him go the ranks of angels, with all the principalities and powers; the cherubim full of eyes and the six-winged seraphim covering their faces and chanting their hymns. Alleluia. Alleluia. Alleluia."*

Truly the hymns and prayers of the liturgy proclaim the real theology of our Church. No wonder the Church Fathers believed that the real theologian is one who prays.

Metropolitan Emilianos Timiadis has written concerning the hymns of our Church: "No church so lavishly employs poetry as does the Eastern Orthodox. The fact that poetry constitutes three-fourths of the Divine Liturgy accounts in a large part for its powerful emotional and aesthetic appeal. In the early centuries those poetic sermons called *Kontakia,* set to music and sung, displaced prose sermons and were, therefore, delivered by the deacons from the pulpit after the Scripture readings."[60] Superb poetry was used to sing out the theology of the Church in its magnificent hymns.

The Call To Commitment

The call to commitment is heard several times in each liturgy. The words used are: "Let us commit ourselves and one another and our whole life to Christ as God." This call to commitment is built into the liturgy and is repeatedly directed to us. It reminds us that Christianity is a love affair between God and us. God first gave Himself to us, and we respond by giving ourselves to Him. The bread and wine we offer to God in the liturgy represent us. They stand for us. We are called to place ourselves on the paten with the altar bread. It is our *prosphora,* our offering of self-surrender to God. We offer Him our mind and heart, our soul and body, all that we have and are. We must, as it were, pour our heart out into the chalice with the wine, and put into it all our hopes and fears, our joys and sorrows, our love and adoration, our obedience and commitment—our whole self. For all this is to go to God in the shape of a gift.

That is our portion in the sacrifice of the liturgy: we are to invest meaning into the gifts by offering ourselves. If we do not offer ourselves to God under the elements of bread and wine, then we are not really offering the liturgy as we should. We are not "in on it." The bread and the wine may mean somebody else. But they don't mean us because we haven't done anything to make them mean us. Every liturgy is an invitation to commit ourselves totally to Christ as God.

"Thine Own of Thine Own We Offer to Thee"

In raising the chalice and paten above the holy table the priest offers us to God through our offering of bread and wine. He says, "Thine own of thine own we offer to Thee," "ta sa ek ton son Si prosferomen." This prayer is taken from I Chronicles 29:14 where we read, "hoti sa ta panta kai ek ton son dedokamen soi." The background here is interesting. King David had gathered an enormous amount of materials in donations for the construction of the temple. In order to discourage any feeling of false pride in the greatness of their gift to God, he acknowledges publicly that what they have contributed to God for the construction of the temple is already God's own gift to them. They are merely giving back to God what He has already given to them. So David says, "But who am I, and what is my people that we should be able thus to offer willingly? For all things come from Thee, and of Thy own have we given Thee." We kneel humbly after this prayer, acknowledging that even in the giving of ourselves to Christ as God, we are merely giving back to Him what He has already given to us.

The Bible and the Liturgy

There has been a tendency among some of our people to separate the Bible and the Liturgy. According to this school of thought, the Bible is Protestant and the liturgy is Orthodox. Nothing could be further from the truth. The Bible is an integral part of the Liturgy and the Liturgy of the Bible. Studies have shown that the liturgy itself has 98 Old Testament quotes and 114 New Testament references. The liturgy is firmly anchored and deeply rooted in Scripture. For, what is the liturgy but a making present again of the events of Scripture? The liturgy unfolds the Scriptures in action. In the Orthodox Church the doctrine of the atonement as we have said, is a liturgical doctrine. Calvary is made present in Baptism and the Eucharist. For example, the passing through the Red Sea becomes real for us today when we pass through the waters of baptism from death to life, from darkness to light, from slavery to freedom. The Ascension becomes our ascension to the throne of God in every liturgy. The manna God provided for His people in the wilderness, He continues to provide for us in the the Eucharist. The Last Supper becomes real for us in every liturgy and we are there with Christ. Thus, the liturgy becomes a bridge, as it were, bringing the events of the Scriptures to us today so that we may participate in them personally, for our salvation and union with God.

In fact, the whole first part of the liturgy is called the Liturgy of the Word since it consists of the reading of the epistle and gospel and their explanation in the sermon. In the early Church the whole first part of the liturgy was dedicated to the preaching of the Scriptures to the unbelievers and the preparation of the catechumens for baptism. Since preaching begets and builds up faith for the faithful also, it continues to be an essential part of the liturgy. According to the Church Fathers, there are two communions in the liturgy. We commune first with Christ as the word of God (Liturgy of the Word), and then with Christ as the Bread of Life (Liturgy of the Faithful). In both communions, we partake of Christ. First we break the word of God, then we break the Bread of Life. The Bible and the liturgy are wedded together inseparably in the services of the Orthodox Church. Through the liturgy the Lord Jesus continues to address His saving word to us. He continues to offer Himself to us completely as both the Word of God and the Bread of Life.

——— The Kiss of Peace: Forgiveness and Love ———

In the Orthodox liturgy love precedes confession of faith. Before we make our confession of faith by reciting the Nicene Creed, we are called upon to "love one another that we may with one mind confess." After the mutual confession of sins the priest says, "Christ is in our midst" and the deacon replies, "He is and ever will be." Commenting on these words Nicolai Gogol writes in his "Meditations on the Divine Liturgy:

"Formerly all those assembled in the church used to kiss one another, men the men and women the women, saying: 'Christ is in the midst of us!' and answering: 'He is and will be!' That tradition persists, though in a modified form, for every communicant summons to his mind all Christians, not only those in the temple at the time, but the absent ones also, not only those close to his heart, but also those who have remained remote from it; hastening to reconcile himself with all those toward whom he has felt envy, hatred or discontent, he gives them all a kiss in spirit, saying to himself: 'Christ is in the midst of us,' and answering on their behalf: 'He is and will be!' Unless he does this he will be dead to all the holy acts that follow, after the words of Christ Himself: 'Leave your gift there before the altar and go; first be reconciled to your brother, and then come and offer your gift;' and after the words of Christ's apostle: 'If any one says, 'I love God,' and hates his brother, he is a liar; for he who does not love his brother whom he has seen, cannot love God whom he has not seen.'"

This call to love that precedes the recitation of the Creed shows that there can be no confession of faith in the Trinity unless it is preceded by mutual love. The true confession of faith must be animated by love.

The Holy Gifts For the Holy

As the priest lifts the consecrated Bread he says, "The Holy Gifts to the holy (people of God)." He does not say, "The Holy Gifts to the *sinless*" or "The Holy Gifts to the *perfect*" because none of us is sinless or perfect. He says ". . . to the *holy* (people of God)." "Holy," of course, means those who are in the process of separating themselves from the sinful world around them and conforming their lives to the will of the One Holy God. Such holiness can never be achieved without the power of the precious Body and Blood of Jesus in us.

Fr. Schmemann emphasizes the word GIFTS: "The holy GIFTS to the holy people of God" and writes,

> *"No one has been 'worthy' to receive communion, no one has been prepared for it. At this point all merits, all righteousness, all devotions disappear and dissolve. Life comes again to us as a Gift, a free and Divine gift. This is why in the Orthodox Church we call the eucharistic elements Holy Gifts. Adam is again introduced into Paradise, taken out of nothingness and crowned king of creation. Everything is free, nothing is due and yet all is given. And, therefore, the greatest humility and obedience is to* accept *the gift, to say* yes — *in joy and gratitude. There is nothing we can do, yet we become all that God wanted us to be from eternity, when we become eucharistic."* [61]

The Long Services

The Orthodox worship services are noted for their length. By contrast, the services of the Western Churches are far shorter. Commenting on this, one anonymous observer wrote:

> *"And the piling up of service after service, repetition, psalm after psalm, has the same effect on the worshipper's awareness of time. The service ceases to be long; it becomes eternal. One ceases to be at a certain place in it, it is simply continuing, as the service of God by the angels and the saints has always continued from the beginning of time and continues now and forever and to ages of ages. Thus beyond*

> *space and time the worshipper is given . . . the experience of what he believes to be reality*—the unending worship of God."

Eucharist — A Sacrifice of Thanksgiving

The prayers of the liturgy reflect the spirit of *thanksgiving* that pervades it:

> *"It is meet and right to sing praises unto Thee, to bless Thee, to magnify Thee, to give thanks unto Thee, to worship Thee in all places of Thy dominion. . . . Thou didst bring us from nothingness into being; and didst raise us up that were fallen away; and left nothing undone till Thou hadst lifted us to heaven, and hadst bestowed upon us Thy kingdom to come . . ."*

We offer thanks to the most Holy Trinity "for all things of which we know and of which we know not, whether manifest or unseen" that God has done for us. Especially do we offer thanks "for this Liturgy, which Thou dost deign to receive at our hands, though there stand by Thee hosts of archangels and tens of thousands of angels waiting upon Thee, the many-eyed cherubim and the six-winged seraphim that soar aloft." We continue our eucharist to God praying, "Holy and most holy art Thou, and Thine only-begotten Son, and Thy Holy Spirit . . . Who so loved the world that Thou didst give Thine only-begotten Son, that whosoever believeth in Him should not perish but have everlasting life." Thus, remembering all that God has done for us from creation when He brought us from non-being into being, through the Incarnation and all the way to the Second Coming of Christ, the Church offers thanksgiving in the anaphora of the liturgy.

The Creed

In the liturgy Christ is Present to speak to us the same words of eternal life He spoke to His apostles. How well this is brought out in the prayer preparatory to the reading of the gospel in the Coptic liturgy:

> *"Lord Jesus Christ our God, who didst say to the saintly disciples and holy apostles, 'Many prophets and righteous people have desired to see the things*

which you see and have not seen them, and to hear the things which you hear and have not heard them; but you, blessed are your eyes for they see and your ears for they hear': make us worthy to hear and to do thy holy gospel through the prayers of the saints.'

In every liturgy we are summoned to renew our baptismal pledge and commitment to Christ. This is the meaning of the Nicene Creed which was introduced into the liturgy in the early sixth century. It was introduced into the liturgy from the baptismal service. Dr. Geoffrey Wainwright says, ". . . The faith confessed in baptism is now being professed again. . . . It expresses the faith which the church proposes for the world's belief and salvation, and its acceptance signifies membership of the saved and saving community. The address of the Creed is to the world, at least in the sense that it reminds believers of the faith by which they entered the church and which they are now charged to spread among humanity."[62]

It is this faith alone that can save humanity. As Dr. John Turkevich, a distinguished Orthodox scientist and priest, wrote, "This is where man stands now after twenty billion years of physical time; after four billion years of biological time; after forty thousand years of theological time; and after two thousand years of Christian time. He stands at the brink of nuclear destruction. Science cannot save him. His only salvation is a miracle based on faith." That miracle is the faith of the Nicene Creed that we confess in each liturgy. It alone offers the way of the salvation and the transfiguration of the cosmos.

The Anaphora

Three of my favorite exhortations from the liturgy are: "Let us love one another," "Let us lift up our hearts," and "Let us give thanks to the Lord." These are part of the anaphora, the upward movement of the soul to God that occurs in the last part of the liturgy. Everywhere around us there is movement. There is constant movement among the celestial bodies in the universe. The multitude of cells and organs in our bodies are constantly moving. The direction of this movement is either up or down, either up to God or away from God. The anaphora is the great thanksgiving prayer of the liturgy that lifts us up to God, climbing Mt. Tabor with Jesus to experience the Transfiguration, reminding us that we are pilgrims passing through this life on our way to heaven. "Let us lift up our hearts." All the movement in our lives—both physical and spiritual—should be toward God. "If you are risen with Christ, seek the things that are above," writes St. Paul. When I lift up my arms and look at the Pantocrator Christ during the anaphora to say, "Let us lift up our hearts," I consider the moment when I shall appear before Him either at my death or at the Second Coming and I pray the prayer of the anaphora with a contrite and joyful heart:

> *We therefore, remembering this saving commandment and all the things that were done for us; the cross, the tomb, the resurrection on the third day, the ascension into heaven, the session at the right hand, the second and glorious coming again; offering you your own from your own, in all and through all; we offer you also this reasonable and bloodless sacrifice, and we beseech and pray and entreat you, send down your Holy Spirit on us and on these gifts set forth; and make this bread the precious body of your Christ, changing it by your Holy Spirit, and that which is in the cup the precious blood of your Christ, changing it by your Holy Spirit, so that they may become to those who partake for vigilance of soul, for forgiveness of sins, for fellowship with the Holy Spirit, for the fullness of the kingdom, for boldness towards you and not for judgement or for condemnation.*

One Body

The liturgy takes us as a human body and transforms us into the mystical body of Christ—the body through which the Risen Christ is present and works in the world today. This is accomplished at the epiclesis when the Holy Spirit comes to abide in us making us Temples of His Presence, and changes the bread and wine into the Body and Blood of Jesus so that, partaking of them, we may become the Body of Jesus in the world today. We literally become His hands, His feet, His ears, His eyes in the world today. "And grant us with *one* mind and *one* heart to glorify and praise Thy sublime and wondrous name . . ." These words remind us that through the Eucharist we indeed become one mind, one heart and one body.

The Inrush of Eternal Life

The liturgy is the inrush of eternal life into us. We receive divine life—God's life—within us here and now. It is the Messianic banquet in which we shall participate fully at the end of time. It introduces us to the kingdom of God.

More than a sacred drama, the liturgy is the experience of the risen Christ in our midst. We celebrate the whole mystery of God's love from creation to the Second Coming. We experience the presence of the reigning Christ. He comes to make His home in us. The words of Jesus are fulfilled: "If a man loves me, he will keep my word, and my Father will love him, and we will come to him and make our home with him" (John 14:23).

In the words of Dr. Geoffrey Wainwright: "Christ's coming to us in communion is the sacramental response to the cry of *Maranatha,* 'Our Lord, come;' it is the anticipation of his final parousia. Those who admit him in faith, who receive him into the very marrow of their bones, are being made 'partakers of divine nature'" (2 Peter 1:4).

The Holy Gifts

"The holy gifts for the holy people of God" says the priest as he invites us to the holy table. The people respond immediately to the words, "The holy gifts to the holy people of God"—No, Lord, we are not holy: "One only is holy, One only is Lord. Jesus Christ to the glory of God the Father. Amen." Regardless of all our human efforts, salvation remains God's gift to us. In the end we simply receive the Eucharist as a gift of God's grace. As the post-communion hymn says,

> "We have seen the true light,
> We have received the heavenly Spirit,
> We have found the true faith,
> We worship the undivided Trinity;
> This has been our salvation."

Our Daily Bread

The Eucharist is God's response to our petition in the Lord's Prayer, "Give us this day our daily bread." Many church Fathers identify "the daily bread" with the bread of life in the Eucharist.

Jesus said, "I am the bread of life; he who comes to me shall not hunger, and he who believes in me shall never thirst . . . your fathers ate the manna in the wilderness and they died. This is the bread which comes down from heaven, that a man may eat of it and not die. I am the living bread which comes down from heaven; if anyone eats of this bread, he will live for ever; and the bread which I shall give for the life of the world is my flesh. . . . He who eats my flesh and drinks my blood abides in me and I live in Him" (John 6:35, 49-51, 56).

A devout Christian who had missed receiving Communion one Sunday thought to himself: "There was a cup set for me at the Lord's Table today, just like the place set for me at the family table at home. The cup was there for me even when I didn't come. When I don't come, my place at the Lord's Table, reserved especially for me, remains empty. And the Lord Jesus, the Host, Who prepares the table for me, must be truly disappointed that one of His invited guests did not show up." As he thought about this, he said, "My place at the Lord's Table will never be empty again—not if I can help it."

A wonderful little pamphlet published by Conciliar Press emphasizes the importance of the liturgy in its answer to the request we so often hear: "Give me one good reason why I should go to church":

"There is one reason above all others why you should go. It is the only place where you can receive Holy Communion.

"*Communion?* Why on earth do we need Communion?

"For one thing . . . faith in Christ will not work and cannot work the way it's supposed to for you or anyone else, without Holy Communion. It is a fact of life that none of us has the strength to fulfill our part in being a Christian without receiving the grace God gives us in Communion.

"Call it Communion, the Eucharist, or the Lord's Supper, you need to be there front and center with faith to receive this indispensable element for a stable Christian life—the Body and Blood of Jesus Christ. It is wishful thinking to attempt living successfully as a Christian without it. Jesus Christ never intended you or anyone else to attempt Christian living without being dynamically united to Him. . . .

"Communion is *the* constant you get from Church. Granted, you can go away with nothing from a bad sermon. But it is totally, completely and irrevocably impossible to receive the body and blood of Jesus Christ and go away with nothing. Quite to the contrary, what could be more life strengthening than receiving the Son of God who became a human being for our sakes so that we could be energized by Him! That's what you do in Communion. You can only get that in Church."[63]

Getting Something Out of the Liturgy

"I DON'T GET ANYTHING OUT OF THE LITURGY." As a priest, I have heard this complaint countless times. The truth is that we do not come to church primarily to get something out of the liturgy. We come to the liturgy to give ourselves, our possessions, our whole being to God. This is what we do when we place ourselves on the holy table through the prosphora, or altar bread, which expresses the giving of our life to God. Only if we first give ourselves to God, shall we be able to get something out of the liturgy. What we will get is the presence of the Lord Jesus within us. We shall carry Him out of the church with us to bring Him as Christ-bearers to others. What we get out of the liturgy is the inestimable privilege of glorifying God and confessing Him among men and women in the world.

Saying, "I don't get anything out of the liturgy" is like showing up at a savings bank and trying to draw out some money when you have not deposited any. What we get out of the liturgy is directly related to what we put into it. The liturgy will be far more meaningful if we participate in the prayers and the singing, the reading of the Gospel beforehand, praying the pre-Communion prayers, the real surrender of ourselves to Christ as God.

Come To the Right Address

The world today is seeking spiritual fulfillment at the wrong address. It seeks fulfillment in alcohol, in drugs, in sex, in work, in hedonism. But it seeks them at the wrong address. The apostles on Pentecost came to the right address: the Upper Room, the same room where Jesus instituted the Eucharist. In that same room on Pentecost—they were so filled with zest that they were accused of being drunk. But they weren't drunk. They were intoxicated. They were intoxicated with God's indwelling Spirit. They were filled with the Spirit Christ had promised to send. We come to the liturgy to receive what gives us life, not what, like drugs, deprives us of life. In coming to the liturgy, we come to the right address if we are seeking the fulfillment that comes only from the fullness of God's presence in us.

Participating in the Liturgy Through Response and Song

When a famous football coach was asked what the contribution of football was to physical fitness, he replied, "Absolutely nothing. I define football as twenty-two men on the field desperately needing rest and sixty thousand people in the stands desperately needing exercise."

This pretty much describes much of the Orthodox worship. Even though the word "liturgy" means *"the work of the people,"* it has become a work no longer of the people but of a few choir members and the priest. The prayers of the liturgy are all in the plural "we." *We* are all offering the liturgy—the whole people of God—not just the priest and the choir. *We* offer, *we* thank, *we* pray, *we* adore, *we* receive.

The Amen of God's People

Fr. Schmemann found a wonderful illustration of the co-celebration of the liturgy by priest and people in the word *Amen:* ". . . it is a crucial word. No prayer, no sacrifice, no blessing is ever given in the Church without being sanctioned by the Amen (of the people) which means an approval, agreement, participation. To say *Amen* to anything means that I make it mine, that I give my consent to it. . . . And *Amen* is indeed the word of the laity in the Church, expressing the function of the laity as the People of God, which freely and joyfully accepts the Divine offer, sanctions it with its consent. There is really no service, no liturgy without the *Amen* of those who have been ordained to serve God as community, as Church."[64]

Personally Involved

The word *amen* means, "I am personally involved in this worship. It is my worship. These are my prayers to God." When we beseech God the Father during the anaphora (the consecration of the bread and wine) to "make this bread the precious body of thy Christ" and "that which is in this cup the precious blood of thy Christ," it is the lay people who must respond with the *Amen* three times. In describing the "Amens" used in the church gatherings of his time, St. Jerome mentions that they were so powerful coming out of so many mouths that when they were pronounced "they sound like thunder and thunderbolts under the existing roofs of the churches." When the priest prays this prayer today, there is almost total silence. In other words, the people of God are not sanctioning this prayer request with their own *Amen*. They are either indifferent or so absorbed in their own private prayers that they are not participating in the prayers of the liturgy.

Praying Together As God's People

Let me share with you what Fr. Thomas Hopko wrote on this subject:

> *"When we go to church to pray, we do not go there to say our private prayers. Our private prayers should be said at home, in our room, in secret, and not in church (Matthew 6:5-6). This does not mean that we do not bring our personal cares, desires, troubles, questions and joys to the prayer of the Church. We certainly can, and we do. But we bring ourselves and our concerns to church to unite them to the prayer of the Church.*
>
> *In church we pray with others, and we should therefore discipline ourselves to pray all together as one body in the unity of one mind, one heart and one soul. Once again this does not mean that our prayers in church should cease to be personal and unique; we must definitely put ourselves into our church prayer. In the Church, however, each one must put his own person with his own personal uniqueness into the common prayer of Christ and His Body. . . . The*

difficulty of many church services is that they are prayers of isolated individuals who are only physically, and not spiritually, united together. . . . The church services are not designed for silent prayer. They exist for the prayerful fellowship of all God's people with each other, with Christ and with God.'' [65]

Put Yourself Into the Liturgy

The liturgy is so structured that it leaves room for people to bring into it their entire existence so that it may be gathered and offered up in praise to God. For example, when the priest asks us to pray for "the peace of the world" we may personalize this prayer and pray briefly at this point for God's peace to prevail in our personal unpeaceful relationships with our wife, husband, children, etc., and then respond with the "Kyrie, eleison." The fact of the matter is that in the petitions of the liturgy, the priest is not addressing himself to God when he says, "Let us pray for the peace of the world . . ." He is speaking to the congregation. He is asking God's people to pray for peace, for unity, for the suffering, etc. If God's people do not pray for those things when the priest directs, but are thinking of something else, then nobody is praying, nothing is being done in the liturgy. That is why we emphasize that the liturgy is not for private prayer. It is the people of God praying together—uniting their requests and offering them up to God in unison, with one mind and one heart.

Here is another example. When we are all kneeling at the anaphora and praying for the Holy Spirit to fill us with His powerful presence and to change our gifts of bread and wine into the body and blood of Jesus, we must not at that time be absorbed in our own personal prayers. This is not the time for private prayer. It is the time for us to pray specifically for the infilling of the Spirit, time for us to shout our *Amen* as we hear the words: "And make this bread the precious body of thy Christ." *Amen!* "And that which is in this cup the precious blood of thy Christ." *Amen!* "Changing them by Thy Holy Spirit." *Amen! Amen! Amen!* What we are in effect saying is: "So be it, Heavenly Father. This is my prayer, my fervent request. Let Your Holy Spirit come upon us and upon these gifts to change them into the precious body and blood of Jesus." If we really pray this prayer, the result will be a new Pentecost, a new and powerful experience of God's presence in us.

In fact, the Emperor Justinian in the fifth Century A.D., decreed that the clergy pray the usually silent prayer of the anaphora or consecration with a louder voice so that the worshippers may be able to hear and respond with the triple *Amen.*

Participate By Singing

Another way by which we are invited to participate in the liturgy is by singing the hymns—not all, of course. There are some hymns that require a specialized choir. But from the earliest years the faithful have always sung the "Amens" and the other dialogue responses such as "Lord, have mercy," "To Thee, O Lord," "Grant this, O Lord," "And with your spirit," etc.

Theophan the Recluse, the great 19th Century bishop and spiritual writer, said:

> *"The purpose of church songs is precisely to make the spark of grace that is hidden within us burn brighter and with greater warmth. This spark is given by the Sacraments. Psalms, hymns, and spiritual odes are introduced to fan the spark and transform it into a flame . . ."*

That is the purpose of singing: to fan the spark of faith and turn it into a flame! St. Augustine said, "He who sings prays twice." Why shouldn't man sing? Is he not "the cantor of the universe" in the words of Abraham Heschel? Is it not the entire universe that praises God when man—the masterpiece of God's creation—stands up to sing praises to God? Doesn't all music begin with God? Who placed those beautiful songs in the birds? Who created the joy of our salvation? Doesn't our baptismal prayer say, "All creation *sang* to Thee when Thou didst appear among us?" Who places a song in our heart when He releases us from the burden of guilt? Why is it that we sing? Is it not because the joy God pours into our hearts through His resurrection is so great that we cannot merely say it with words; we have to sing it out? When Joseph Haydn, the great composer, was being criticized for the gaiety of his church music, he replied, "I cannot help it. I give forth what is in me. When I think of God, my heart is so full of joy that the notes fly off as from a spindle . . ."

We Participate By Hearing the "Secret" Prayers

Archbishop Paul of Finland writes:

"In the early Church all the prayers of the Liturgy were read aloud. The whole congregation participated in them. But as early as the sixth century some of the prayers of the Liturgy began to be read in a low voice by the celebrating priest. Although there were attempts to oppose this change, it gradually became the general practice, so that the handbook still indicates which parts of the prayers in the Liturgy are to be read 'secretly,' by the priest alone. However, insofar as there has been an effort to deepen the congregation's understanding of the Liturgy, it has now been found necessary to go back to the practice of reading the prayers of the Liturgy aloud.

"How can the whole assembly of God's people participate in the sacrament of redemption with full understanding and true feeling and realize that they are a royal priesthood bringing spiritual offerings, if they hear only fragments or closing sentences of the common prayers without being aware of their meaning as a whole?" [66]

The Devil Has Nothing to Sing About

It is no wonder someone said once, "Christianity came into the world on wings of song. Infidelity never sings. Unbelief has no music, no anthems, no hymns, no oratorios or symphonies." When Robert Ingersoll, an agnostic, died, the printed notice of his funeral stated, "There will be no singing." Atheism and agnosticism have nothing to sing about. One great Christian said, "The devil hates music because he cannot stand gaiety. Satan can smirk but he cannot laugh; he can sneer but he cannot sing." He has nothing to sing about!

Kirchoff said of the beautiful hymns of the Eastern Church:

"As in heaven the singing of the angels rings out and soars around the exalted majesty of God . . . in the same way the Eastern Church is convinced that the service she offers God's majesty is the same as that of

the angels . . . that her hymns are modeled on those of the angels, an echo of the everlasting song of the cherubim." [67]

———— Who Sang in the Early Church? ————

But who sings these beautiful hymns of the angels? Fr. Alexander Elchaninov answers, "Few even realize that the so-called 'choir' speaks and sings in the name of the entire congregation, and that in the early Church there were none of those specially trained, professional singers who now perform this 'duty.' All sang, testifying *their own faith* . . ." We sing to testify, to express our own faith, and to fan that spark of grace into a flame.

We sing as the apostles sang. After hearing of their Lord's imminent suffering and death, we read in Matthew that "they sang a hymn and went out to the Mount of Olives." There was no choir there to sing for them. They were the choir. And as they left the Upper Room that night and crossed the brook Kidron, again they sang a hymn. The Apostle Paul sang in prison at midnight. The apostles sang in joy and they sang in sorrow. They sang because God had put a song—the song of the resurrection—in their hearts.

———— We Heard No Music ————

There is a story of some monks in France who were known and loved for their great sympathy and kind deeds; but not one of them could sing. Try as they would, the music in their services was a failure, and it became a great grief to them that only in their hearts could they "make melody to the Lord."

One day a traveling monk, who was a great singer, asked for lodging. They were overjoyed, for now they could have him sing for their services, and they planned to keep him with them always.

But that night an angel appeared to the abbot in a dream, "Why was there no music in your chapel tonight? We angels always listen for the beautiful music that rises from your services."

"You must be mistaken!" cried the abbot, "Usually we have no music worth hearing; but tonight we had a trained singer with a wonderful voice, and he sang the service for us. For the first time in all these years our music was beautiful." The angel smiled. "And yet up in heaven we heard nothing," he said softly.

A Personal Testimony

May I conclude by sharing with you the personal testimony of a Presbyterian mother who visited the Soviet Union in 1984:

"I must admit to you that I set out on this journey for selfish reasons—to satisfy a life-long desire to see the Soviet Union to dispel some myths for my children when they ask. It's funny how the Holy Spirit works (remember I was worshipping in the center of the Russian Orthodox Church on Pentecost!). I came home with a deeper spirituality and sense of inner peace than I have been consciously aware of. I attended Orthodox liturgy daily and each day my involvement became more intense.

"For Russian Orthodox Christians, the Divine Liturgy is a meeting place between heaven and earth; an area of life in which men and women commune with God. It is celebrated with a fervor that is uninhibited, yet not hysterical. The liturgy is performed in the Old Church Slavonic—a language the average Russian can neither theologically nor linguistically understand (nor could I!). The image of God is powerfully communicated by a synthesis of poetry, paintings, drama and music. It totally encompasses all 5 senses. Imagine, if you will, standing body to body with hundreds of people, immobilized for 2-3 hours. Smell the sweet incense surrounding you as the image of God. Hear the crackling tapers tended by babushka. There are birds chirping outside and sunbeams streaming through the onion dome. Feel the intense gaze of the icons sharing in the worship with you. How melodious Russian congregations sing without any musical accompaniment. Massed soprano voices, pure without training. You are hearing the angels sing! Imagine whispering in English the Creed, Gloria and Lord's Prayer while the congregation chants them in the Old Church Slavonic. I cried everytime.

"I was anointed with a delicately fragranced oil to reconfirm my Baptism at Our Lady of Kazan Cathedral in Volgograd. As non-Orthodox, we were unable to receive the Holy Eucharist. That was very painful not to participate in a full union with my Orthodox brothers and sisters.

"Soviet society can offer no comparable calm or beauty to the Orthodox liturgy. I suggest the same is true for our society. Peace is invoked, requested and exchanged several times during the Divine Liturgy. Peace is not merely the absence of conflict, but the presence of that Divine Person whose very being is order, harmony, joy, life, creation; and whose absence is emptiness, nothingness and chaos. This is made present in sight, sound, touch, taste, word and action each time the liturgy is celebrated. Through this, Orthodox Christians discover and receive the peace of God which passes all human understanding.''

Chapter **12**

Epiphany and the Blessing of Water

Water! What an amazing gift! A few drops lift up a plant's drooping leaves, or refresh a human body. You can wash in it, splash in it, swim in it. You can relish in its sounds—the babble of a brook or the roaring of the sea, or the breaking of the waves upon the sandy beach. Life springs from water. Not just physical life but spiritual life as well. For we are born anew in baptism of water and the Spirit.

Partly because we take water for granted, partly because it's cheaper than dirt (in most cities a ton of water delivered to your kitchen costs about 15 cents), we use it lavishly. We each draw about 87 gallons a day: 24 for flushing, 32 for bathing, laundry, and dishwashing, and 25 for swimming pools and watering the lawn. We use only two gallons a day for drinking and cooking—the only water we actually require in order to survive.

But this is just the beginning. An immense amount of water is needed for irrigation and industrial use. For example, the eggs you ate for breakfast this morning required 120 gallons of water each; the steak you might have for dinner, 3,500 gallons; the ton of steel in your car 60,000 gallons. When we consider these indirect uses of water, our daily need soars to 2,000 gallons each day for each person.

Not Running Out

Despite this staggering use of water, experts do not think we'll be running out of water. They tell us that four trillion gallons of rain water falls on the United States each day and that we use a mere tenth of it. Most of this one tenth returns to its source. The rest escapes into the atmosphere, but only briefly. None is lost; the water that St. John used to baptize Jesus still exists. Its billions of molecules are now dispersed throughout the world.

Water is absolutely essential to human life. It carries blood through the 60,000 miles of arteries, capillaries and veins in our bodies. It is necessary for digestion. It lubricates our joints, keeps mucous membranes moist, and enables our eyes to function. It regulates our body heat, and it is essential to all plant and animal life, which are so important to human survival.

Modern science has discovered that all of life on earth came out of water. In primeval times, all life, including ours, was in the sea. Modern obstetrics has shown that the human embryo is born from the amniotic fluid in the mother's womb, and that this fluid has the same composition as sea water.

Primordial Element

Tertullian talks of water as the primordial element in which life appears: "First of all, O man, you should have reverence for the antiquity of the waters as a primordial element. . . . Once the elements of the world were set in order, when it was to be given inhabitants, it was the primordial waters which were commanded to produce living creatures. The primordial water brought forth life, so that no one should be astonished that in Baptism the waters are able to give life" (Bapt. 2). Tertullian bases these words on Genesis I where water is indeed the primordial element in creation.

How beautiful is the metaphor Jesus used so often: "the water of life." Water is life! As the body must have water, so the soul must have the water of life. The Bible closes with an invitation to drink of that water: "Whosoever will, let him take the water of life freely" (Rev. 22:17).

Why Water as a Means of Grace?

Speaking on the use of water as a means of grace, St. Cyril of Jerusalem wrote: "If you wish to know why it is by means of water and not some other element that grace is given, you will find the reason in going through the Scriptures. Water is a wonderful thing:—and the most beautiful of the four sensible elements of the cosmos. The sky is the dwelling of the angels, but the skies are made of water; earth is the home of men, but the earth has come out of the waters; and before the creation of visible things in six days, the Spirit of God hovered over the waters. The water is the principle of the Cosmos, and the Jordan of the Gospel" (XXXIII, 433A).

Tertullian says that as the primordial waters of creation begot the fish, the baptismal water begets "little fishes" or "little Christs." He writes in *De Baptismo:* "We are little fishes according to *the ichthys* (FISH), Jesus Christ, in Whom we are born, and we only live by remaining in the water" (De Bapt. I).

It is clear why the Church uses water as a sign of the divine life of grace. We rise from the waters of baptism into a new life, born again of water and the Spirit. In those same waters the old nature is drowned and put to death. The creative as well as the destructive element in water expresses powerfully what God does for us in the waters of baptism.

The Blessing of Water

The blessing of water through prayer and the invocation of the Holy Spirit, with the immersion in the water of a small ceremonial cross, had been introduced into liturgical use in the fourth century. Through sprinkling, by sealing with the sign of the cross and by drinking of the blest water, the faithful are cleansed and sanctified. The sanctified water was used for the healing of soul and body, and for protection against evil. Gradually it came to be used even for the healing of sick animals and for the blessing of God on new homes and buildings. The Church prays in this Rite of the Blessing of the Waters: "that those who sprinkle and partake thereof (of the Holy Water) may receive it for the cleansing of souls and bodies, for the healing of sickness, for the sanctification of houses, and sufficient for every need."

At Epiphany the Church prays over the water as it does at every baptism:

"Therefore, O King who loves mankind, do Thou Thyself be present now as then through the descent of Thy Holy Spirit, and sanctify this water."

"Confer upon it the grace of redemption, the blessing of the Jordan. Make it a . . . gift of sanctification, a remission of sins, a protection against disease, a destruction to demons . . . filled with angelic strength: that all who draw from it and partake of it may have it for the cleansing of their soul and body . . . for the sanctification of their dwellings . . ."

The baptismal water as well as the water that is distributed on Epiphany is blessed by a prayer which recalls beautifully all the events of salvation which were in any way connected with water, from the beginning of our world when God's Spirit hovered over the water, down to the commandment of Jesus to baptize.

For example, listen to the words of St. Sophronius:

*"For Thou art our God, Who hast renewed
through water and the Spirit our nature
grown old through sin.*

*Thou art our God Who hast drowned sin
through water in the days of Noah.*

*Thou art our God Who, through the
waters of the sea, at Moses' hand hast set free
the Hebrew nation from
the bondage of Pharoah.*

*Thou art our God Who hast cleft the
rock in the wilderness: the waters
gushed out, the streams overflowed, and
Thou hast satisfied Thy thirsty people.*

*Thou art our God Who by water and
fire through Elijah hast brought
back Israel from the error of Baal."*

In Rev. 22:1-3 we read of the river of the water of life that flows from the throne of God yielding each month twelve kinds of fruit on the trees that lined the river on either side. The leaves of the trees were for the healing of all nations. See also Ezekiel 47:1-12. Note that the river of the water of life has its source at the very throne of God.

The blessed water we receive on Epiphany is like the healing water that flows into our lives from the very throne of God, nourishing our parched souls that they may bear fruit for God's glory.

The Abode of the Serpent

In the ancient Near East, water was considered the home of the monsters of the abyss, the dragons of the depths. It was the abode of the serpent that tempted the first man. God cursed the serpent, but Jesus came to crush its head in the waters of the Jordan, to destroy the abode of sin and death from which man would have to be snatched.

St. Cyril of Jerusalem, in his Catechesis, speaks of the sanctification of all things by the Baptism of Christ. All creation was made holy by the fact that Jesus descended into the waters of the Jordan and the Holy Spirit came down upon Him and upon the waters at the same time, driving out the devil and making them the instrument through which the new creation, the new man in Christ, was to be born.

He writes:

"When, therefore, it was time to crush the head of the dragon, Christ descended into the waters and bound the strong one, in order that we might receive the power to tread upon serpents and scorpions. This was no small beast, but a terrible one, bringing death to all who met him. But life came to our rescue in order that death might be shut up in prison forever, and in order that we might all say: 'O death where is thy victory?' By baptism the sting of death is taken away."

The River Jordan

The river Jordan in which Jesus was baptized is replete with meaning in the history of our salvation. Fr. Thomas Hopko brings this out most effectively when he writes:

The river Jordan plays a very important role in the Bible. Before it becomes the river in which Jesus the Messiah is baptized, it is revealed as the river which bounds the "promised land." To cross the Jordan, for the people of Israel, was to enter into the fulfillment of the Lord's promises. It was to enter into the "land flowing with milk and honey," the place where God would dwell with His people providing them with the endless blessings of His presence.

In the New Testament, with its spiritual and mystical fulfillment of the Old, to cross the Jordan was to enter into the Kingdom of God, to experience the fullness of the life of the age to come. The fact that Moses was not blessed to cross the Jordan thus became a symbol of the fact that the Law by itself could not save Israel or the world. It had to be Joshua, which literally means Savior, and is the Hebrew form of the Greek word Jesus, who leads the people across the Jordan and into the promised land, thus symbolizing the saving action of the new Joshua, Jesus the messianic Savior, in the covenant of grace. . . .

The river Jordan was also parted by the passage of Elijah and Elisha, an event also recalled at the liturgy of Epiphany (2 Kings 2). And it was from the Jordan that Elijah was taken up into heaven in order to return again, as the tradition developed, to prepare the way for the coming of the Messiah (See Matt. 17:9-13). It was also in the Jordan that Naaman the Syrian was cleansed from his leprosy, a sign referred to by Jesus as a prefiguration of the salvation of all people, not only those of Israel (Lk 4:27). In the account of Naaman's cure the special significance of the Jordan is stressed once again (2 Kings 5:10-14). . . .

Can we not be washed in just any river and be clean? God's answer is, No. Only in the Jordan, in the baptism of Christ, are we cleansed from all of our sins. Only through the Jordan do we enter into the land of the living, the promised land of God's kingdom. Only by the sanctified waters of the Jordan does God sanctify us forever.[68]

The Water of Life

Water has been used as a symbol for Jesus. As Jesus said to the Samaritan woman, ''Every one who drinks of this water will thirst again, but whoever drinks of the water I shall give him will never thirst; the water that I shall give him will become in him a spring of water welling up to eternal life'' (John 4:13-14).

The Prophet Jeremiah wrote, ''For my people have committed two evils: they have forsaken me the fountain of living waters, and hewed out cisterns for themselves, broken cisterns that can hold no water" (Jer. 2:13).

The Prophet Jeremiah could not have been more contemporary. The world today has indeed forsaken the fountain and is trying to satisfy its thirst by drinking from the many broken cisterns.

Let us look briefly at man's deep spiritual thirst today.

A Deeper Thirst

Once our physical needs are met, our spiritual thirst remains. We thirst for knowledge. We thirst for the ultimate concerns of life. We thirst for meaning. We thirst to know why the world was created. We thirst to know who we are. We thirst to know our purpose in life. We thirst to know God. We thirst to know if there is an existence beyond death. If we do not in some way answer these questions, the inner thirst grows painful like actual physical thirst. It makes us desperate. It causes suffering and agony. This painful thirst of the soul is what causes a great deal of the dreadful anxiety that exists in the world today.

King Tantalus

In Greek mythology, King Tantalus was punished in the underworld by being chained in a lake. Its water reached to his chin but withdrew whenever he bent down to satisfy his burning thirst. Over his head were branches laden with choice fruit, but they immediately drew back whenever he reached up to satisfy his hunger. A symbol of utter frustration, his name is immortalized in the English word "tantalize." So, too, seeking to satisfy the inner thirst of the soul apart from Christ is tantalizing, utterly futile.

Everything in this world that we use to try to satisfy the thirst of the soul—money, lust, drugs, possessions, fame—is like a broken cistern. It cannot hold the water that is poured into it. And the thirst only grows worse as a result. One would think that these broken cisterns would drive us to the fountain of living waters. But it doesn't happen, because we allow ourselves to be satisfied with those broken cisterns. We need to pray that the Lord not allow us to be satisfied with the tantalizing things of this world that serve only to increase our thirst. "Anyone who drinks of this water will thirst again," said Jesus.

We need to pray that the Lord create a new thirst in us for the real water of life. The old saying goes, "You can lead a horse to water but you cannot make him drink." That is our great problem as priests and preachers of the Church. We try to lead God's people to the water of life, but we cannot make them drink. We cannot create a thirst in them for the water of life. Only God can. We offer them the water of life, and they continue to drink from the broken cisterns of sin. We offer them the clear, crystal, thirst-quenching water of Jesus, and they continue to slake their thirst in the pig pens of the world. We offer them the pure water of Jesus, and they continue trying to satisfy their thirst in the polluted waters of sin.

Nothing will satisfy the burning thirst of tormented souls but to take them to the fountain of living waters, to true fellowship with Christ. ". . . whoever drinks of the water I shall give him will never thirst again," said Jesus, "but the water I shall give him will become a well of water within him that bubbles up to eternal life" (Jn. 4:12). "Ho, everyone who thirsts, come to the waters" (Isaiah 55:1). To make clear where these life-giving waters are to be found, Jesus says, "Come to me all you who labor and are heavy laden and I will give you rest." The water of life, of which if anyone drink, he shall never thirst again, flows from Jesus at the very throne of God: "Then he showed me the river of the water of life, bright as crystal, flowing from the throne of God and of the Lamb . . ." (Rev. 22:1).

Christ came to make us not cisterns but artesian wells. Cisterns cannot stand drought and rainless months, but an artesian well can endure any drought, even parched fields and empty reservoirs, because it has within its own spring that wells up with an endless source of refreshment.

Here then is the true meaning of the holy water we receive every year on Epiphany. It should remind us of Jesus Who is the water of life, Who alone is able to satisfy the deepest thirst of the soul. But the important question is: Is Jesus the Fountain of Living waters for you? Do you come to Him regularly through prayer, through the reading of the Bible, through participation in the Eucharist to let Him satisfy the deep thirst of your soul for meaning and for fellowship with God? Or are you satisfied with quenching your thirst in the broken, brackish cisterns of this world that can hold no water but serve only to increase your thirst?

Jesus said,

> "If any one thirst, let him come to me and drink. He who believes in me, as the scripture has said, 'Out of his heart shall flow rivers of living water" (John 7:37-38).

An artesian well within each believer!

Holy Water: A Symbol of Nature Set Free From Sin

It is Jesus—the Water of Life—Who blessed the waters of the earth when He stepped into the Jordan River to be baptized. As Bishop Kallistos Ware writes:

> "When Christ went down into the waters, not only did He carry us down with Him and make us clean, but He also made clean the nature of the waters themselves. As the troparion of the forefeast puts it, 'Christ has appeared in the Jordan to sanctify the waters.' The feast of Theophany has thus a cosmic aspect. The fall of the angelic orders, and after it the fall of man, involved the whole universe. All God's creation was thereby warped and disfigured: to use the symbolism of the liturgical texts, the waters were made a 'lair of dragons.' Christ came on earth to redeem not only man, but—through man—the entire material creation. When He entered the water, besides effecting by anticipation our rebirth in the font, he likewise effected the cleansing of the waters, their transfiguration into an organ of healing and grace." [69]

Thus, by her consecration of the waters, the Church frees water from the dark and evil powers that reside in it. Holy water becomes the symbol of nature set free from sin and consecrated by the Holy Spirit to our blessing and the blessing of our homes.

The Biblical Theme of Water

A monk of the Eastern Church writes concerning Jesus and water:

> "One of the favourite themes of primitive Christian art is Moses striking the rock with his rod and

causing water to gush out. The water-theme comes over and over again in the Old Testament, from the crossing of the Red Sea by Israel, to Isaiah's call: 'Ho, everyone that thirstest, come ye to the waters . . .' (Isa. 55:1). The fulfillment of these passages of Scripture is to be found in the words of Our Lord reported in the Gospel: 'Except a man be born of Water and of the Spirit, he cannot enter into the Kingdom of God (John 3:5); if any man thirst, let him come unto me and drink. He that believeth on me . . . out of his belly shall flow rivers of living water' (John 7, 37, 38).

Water has become the sign of salvation. Our Lord commanded His disciples to baptize: 'Go ye therefore, and teach all the nations, baptizing them . . .' (Matt. 28:19). He Himself inaugurated His public ministry by receiving the baptism of John. Eastern Fathers, chiefly St. Ignatius of Antioch, teach that the contact of our Lord's body with the water of Jordan is the principle of the sanctifying action of water in the holy mystery of Baptism.' [70]

────────────── **Water and the Eucharist** ──────────────

St. Ambrose compared the water that flowed from the rock in the Old Testament to the Eucharist in the New Testament: "The water flowed from the Rock for the Jews, the Blood of Christ (flows) for you; the water slaked their thirst for an hour, the Blood quenches your thirst forever. The Jews drank and thirsted once more; when you have drunk, you need never thirst again. That (the water from the rock) was a figure; this (the Eucharist) is the truth. If the figure seems wonderful to you, how much more the reality the figure of which you admire" (De Myst. 48; Botte, 123).

Fr. Lev Gillet continues the analogy between water and the Eucharist when he writes, "Water that purifies cannot be thought of apart from Thy Blood. The Blood shed for us, for me. . . . Blood and water poured out together from the side which was pierced by the spear. And thus the mystery of water leads us into the mystery of Blood. The water of Jordan mingles with the Blood of Calvary" (In Thy Presence." SVS Press. Crestwood, NY. p. 87).

The Supernatural Rock: Christ

St. Paul writes about the Rock that yielded water in the wilderness: "I want you to know, brethren, that our fathers were all under the cloud, and all passed through the sea, and all were baptized into Moses in the cloud and in the sea, and all ate the same supernatural food and all drank the same supernatural drink. For they drank from the supernatural Rock which followed them, and the Rock was Christ" (I Cor. 10:1-4). May we drink of this Rock often. For it continues to flow to this day, bringing to us the very presence of Him Who is the Water of Life.

The First and the Second Creation

Just as the Spirit descended upon the waters in the beginning and produced the first creation, so at the moment Jesus was baptized in the Jordan River, the Holy Spirit descended in the form of a dove and hovered over the waters to bring forth from them the second creation, man and woman renewed after the image of their Creator. In this second creation the baptized person is born anew in the waters consecrated by the epiclesis. The result is a new creation and a renewal of the first creation.

The Church Fathers on Water

Concerning the blessing of the water, Theodore of Mopsuestia writes, "First of all the Bishop, according to the law of the pontifical service, should use the prescribed words and ask of God that the grace of the Holy Spirit should come on the water and make it capable of this awe-inspiring birth" (XIV. 9). Cyril of Jerusalem writes, "Ordinary water, by the invocation of the Holy Spirit, of the Son, and of the Father, acquires a sanctifying power" (XXXIII, 429A). Ambrose adds, "You have seen the water, but all water does not heal; that water heals which has the grace of Christ. The water is the instrument, but it is the Holy Spirit Who acts. The water does not heal, if the Spirit does not descend to consecrate it" (De Sacr. 1, 15; Botte 58-59).

Water From the Baptismal Pools

Following the baptismal services that took place on the Feast of the Epiphany in the Early Church, the faithful began taking home some of the water from the baptismal pools, treasuring it for its consecrating and healing powers. St. John Chrysostom wrote about this practice: "On this occasion of the commemoration of the baptism of the Savior on which He sanctified the nature of the water, the people on leaving the church after midnight used to take home some of the water and keep it. It was noticed that this water stays pure and placid for two or three years" (Hom. 24. De Bapt. Christ).

The custom prevailed in the East not only of consecrating water in churches on Epiphany, but also of blessing a nearby river or fountain in honor of Christ's baptism. In Palestine it was the Jordan River that received this blessing in a colorful and solemn ceremony. Thousands of pilgrims would gather on its shores to step into the water after the blessing, submerging three times as they renewed their baptismal vows.

Fr. Alkiviades Calivas notes that, "In earlier times Churches had a fountain in their courtyard. The water contained in the fountain was usually blessed. The faithful were accustomed to drawing water from the fountain and to use it for purposes of sanctification and/or for symbolic washings before they entered the Church. One such famous fountain was the Font of the Church of Holy Wisdom (St. Sophia) in Constantinople, with its unique inscription which in Greek read the same forward and backward (Wash your sins — not only your face). The Services of Agiasmos (Blessing of Water) were usually conducted at these fonts. This custom is still prevalent in monastic communities."

Explanation of the Service

On the Feast of Epiphany, the Church calls us to go to the river Jordan to witness the manifestation of God and the Baptism of our Lord Jesus Christ. There we see, with the eyes of our soul, our Lord immersing Himself once again in the waters of the River Jordan, and thus sanctifying the oceans, rivers and lakes of the world.

On the Feast of Epiphany the priest performs the special Rite of the Blessing of the Waters. He asks our Lord that just as 2,000 years ago He blessed the water in the Jordan River, so today He bless the water that we have before us so that in the words of the prayer: *"those who sprinkle and partake thereof (of the Holy*

Water) may receive it for the cleansing of souls and bodies, for the healing of suffering, for the sanctification of homes, and for every need." Upon leaving church we take a container of holy water home to bless ourselves and our homes. "Today the streams of Jordan are changed into healing waters by the presence of the Lord," says the prayer of Patriarch Sophronius of Jerusalem, recited in the Rite of the Blessing of Waters on Epiphany.

The sprinkling of the people with holy water which takes place during this service has its roots in ancient practices of baptism where it was customary to sprinkle the faithful with the consecrated waters of the baptismal font before the catechumens were baptized.

In some parts of the country an Orthodox bishop throws a cross into a body of water to be retrieved by a swimmer. In the local parish the priest immerses a cross into a vessel containing water. He immerses it three times to recall the triple immersion of Christ in the Jordan, as well as the triple immersion of every Orthodox believer in the baptismal font. This act represents our Lord immersing Himself once again in the River Jordan and sanctifying the rivers and lakes of the world. Thus the consecrated water brings to us the healing presence of the Lord.

Children should be encouraged to keep the small container of holy water which they receive on this day. They can place it by their personal icon and use it the year round. They can use it to bless themselves or their room or their new bicycle, or pet, etc. They can partake of it when they feel they have a special need for the Lord's presence at home. It will represent the Lord's healing and loving presence with them constantly as does the family icon. Thus we can teach our children to keep Epiphany the year round.

Epiphany or Theophany

The meaning of Epiphany is expressed by the word *epiphany* itself which means in Greek the SHOWING FORTH or MANIFESTATION of God. The word THEOPHANY expresses it even better. It means the APPEARANCE of God. Christ's baptism in the Jordan River marks the manifestation of the Triune God to the world. For it was at the baptism of Jesus that God revealed Himself as Father, Son and Holy Spirit. The Holy Trinity was made manifest: the Father testified from on high to the divine

Sonship of Jesus: "This is my beloved Son, in whom I am well pleased;" the Son received His Father's testimony; and the Spirit was seen in the form of a dove, descending from the Father and resting upon the Son. Thus, God revealed Himself fully on Epiphany as the Father Who loves us, the Son Who saves us, the Holy Spirit Who lives in us. As the troparion of the Feast says,

"When Thou, O Lord was baptized in the Jordan,
The worship of the Trinity was made manifest.
For the voice of the Father bore witness unto Thee,
Calling Thee the beloved Son,
And the Spirit in the form of a dove
Confirmed His word as sure and steadfast.
O Christ our God, Who hast appeared and enlightened
*   the world,*
Glory to Thee.

Bishop Kallistos Ware emphasizes that the blessing of the waters on Epiphany "is effected not by the officiating priest and the people who are praying with him, but by Christ Himself, Who is the true celebrant in this as in all mysteries of the Church. It is the Christ who has blessed the waters once for all at His baptism in the Jordan: the liturgical ceremony of blessing is simply an extension of Christ's original act."[71]

Through the blessing of the waters the Church proclaims that the same Jesus Who sanctified the waters in the Jordan River is the One Who sanctifies the fallen world, transforming it into "the new heaven and the new earth" where creation will be "filled with the fullness of God" (Eph. 3:19). The purpose of the casting out of evil mentioned in the Epiphany prayers is that all may be transformed "in Christ." At Epiphany the new creation is inaugurated.

From the Service of the Blessing of Water

The voice of the Lord cries over the waters saying: Come all ye receive the Spirit of wisdom, the Spirit of understanding, the Spirit of the fear of God, even Christ who is made manifest.

Today the nature of water is sanctified. Jordan is divided in two, and turns back the stream of its waters, beholding the Master being baptized.

As a man Thou didst come to that river, O Christ our King, and dost hasten O Good One, to receive the baptism of a servant at the hands of the Forerunner (John), because of our sins, O Lover of Man.

Following are three readings from the Prophecy of Isaiah concerning the messianic age. These are part of the Rite of the Blessing of Water:

Let the thirsty wilderness be glad, let the desert rejoice, let it blossom as a rose, let it blossom abundantly, let everything rejoice . . . (Isaiah 35:1-10).

Go to that water, O you who thirst, and as many as have no money, let them eat and drink without price, both wine and fat . . . (Isaiah 55:1-13).

With joy draw the water out of the wells of salvation. And in that day shall you say: Confess ye unto the Lord and call upon his Name; declare his glorious deeds . . . his Name is exalted . . . Hymn the Name of the Lord . . . Rejoice and exult . . . (Isaiah 12:3-6).

From St. Sophronius:

"Today the grace of the Holy Spirit hath descended on the waters in the likeness of a dove. Today hath shone the Sun that setteth not, and the world is lighted by the light of the Lord. Today the moon shineth with the world in its radiating beams. Today the shining stars adorn the universe with the splendour of their radiance. Today the clouds from heaven moisten mankind with showers of justice.

"Today the waters of the Jordan are changed to healing by the presence of the Lord. Today the whole universe is watered by mystical streams. Today the sins of mankind are blotted out by the waters of the Jordan. Today hath paradise been opened to mankind and the Sun of righteousness hath shone for us.

"Today we have escaped from darkness, and by the light of the knowledge of God we have been illuminated. Today the darkness of the world vanisheth with the appearance of our God. Today the whole creation is lighted from on high. Today we have been purchased for the Kingdom.

> *"Today the Lord cometh to baptism to elevate mankind above.*
>
> *"Today the land and the sea have divided between them the joy of the world, and the world hath been filled with rejoicing.*
>
> *"Today the streams of Jordan are changed into healing waters by the presence of the Lord. . . .*

Elsewhere:

> *Therefore, O King and Lover of mankind, come and sanctify this water through the descent of your Holy Spirit. And confer upon it the grace of redemption, and the blessing of Jordan. Make it a font of incorruptibility, a gift of sanctification, a remission of sins, a healing of sickness, a destroyer of demons, render it inaccessible to the adverse powers, and make it full of the power of Angels, so that all who draw from it and partake of it may be blessed in their souls and bodies, healed of their sufferings, sanctified in their homes, and they may receive every befitting grace. . . . Grant sanctification, blessing, cleansing and health to all those who touch it, who sprinkle themselves with it or partake of it."*

"Come, then, King and Lover of mankind and sanctify this water through the descent of the Holy Spirit," prays the priest.

The prayers of this beautiful rite of the blessing of water invoke the Holy Spirit repeatedly to descend upon the water, purify and sanctify it, and impart to it healing grace. The Great *Synapte* or Litany in this service includes twenty-six prayer requests in the following vein:

> *"that these waters may be sanctified by the power, operation and descent of the Holy Spirit."*
>
> *"that there may descend upon these waters the purifying action of the most substantial Trinity."*
>
> *"that this water may be endowed with the grace of redemption, the blessing of the Jordan, through the power, action and descent of the Holy Spirit."*
>
> *"that it may serve as a purification of the souls and bodies of all those who, with faith, shall draw and partake of it,"* etc.

This last petition shows that the blest water offers healing grace and strength only to those who partake of it with faith; to those who come cleansed in spirit and stand ready to follow Christ as His co-workers in the world. Not all the holy water in the world will be of help to those who come passively, without faith.

"Lord, Wash Me!"

Fr. Lev Gillet in his inspiring devotional book "In His Presence" meditates on the meaning of water as follows: "Thou art not only the giver of water. Thou Thyself, Lord, art this living water. . . . Thou art the water that brings fertility to the arid and parched earth. At the beginning of the day, Thou art the dew which makes my soul able to bear leaves and fruit. . . . When Thou didst take it upon Thyself to wash the feet of Thy disciples and came to Simon Peter, who in humility protested, Thou didst answer him: 'If I wash thee not, thou hast no part with me.' Lord, my whole desire is to have a part with Thee. So, wash me. Wash me completely. I am not like Thy disciples who were already pure: as Thou didst say to them, it was from their feet only that the dust of the road had to be cleansed. Wash Thou my hands and my head. Wash my whole body. Bathe me. Give Thy spotlessness to all which in my thought, in my will, in my emotions, in my senses, needs purifying."[72]

Tears as Water

Continuing his meditation on water, Fr. Gillet speaks of water in the form of tears: "The grace of a second baptism—the baptism of repentance is also symbolized by water. But this time it is the water of tears. Thou didst abase Thyself in front of me, Lord, to wash my feet. And I, with Mary Magdalene, kneel before Thee and, in my turn, wash Thy feet. I wash them with the tears that I shed, or with the tears that I ask for. Have I any tears? Oh, give them to me! Break my heart! This baptism of burning tears, how powerful it is, for it can bring about repeatedly what the first baptism brought about once."

A Renewal of Baptism

On Epiphany we are called to reaffirm our own baptism. For, there is a close connection between the baptism of Jesus on Epiphany and our baptism. As Bishop Kallistos Ware writes,

> *"In Christ's baptism at the hands of John, our own baptismal regeneration is already accomplished by anticipation. The many celebrations of the Eucharist are all a participation in the single and unique Last Supper; and in a similar way all our individual baptisms are a sharing in the baptism of Christ—they are the means whereby the 'grace of Jordan' is extended, so that it may be appropriated by each one of us personally. As an indication of the close connection between Christ's baptism and our baptism, it may be noted that the prayer at the Great Blessing of the Waters on Theophany is almost identical with the prayer of blessing said over the font at the sacrament of baptism."* [73]

Claim the Treasure

A news item told about an express package that reached an address in England from a South African town. The man who was to receive the box refused to pay the delivery charges. Consequently for about fourteen years that unclaimed box was used as a footstool in the express office. One day purely out of curiosity at an auction a man bid for it at a very low price. When he opened it later he was greatly astonished to find several thousand pounds of sterling in English bank notes. Because the original consignee had refused to pay the comparatively small delivery charges, he had missed receiving a small fortune.

People are often just that shortsighted. They deprive themselves of life's richest blessings simply because they fail to claim them. We have within our reach the greatest blessing of all: adoption as sons and daughters of God, all of God's care and protection and love, and life eternal in the presence of God. We have received these blessings through baptism. But many of us have yet to claim this treasure. We are using it as a footstool. We refuse to pay the delivery charges. We refuse to take time for God, to listen to His instructions, to study His word, to repent of our sins, to seek His forgiveness, to receive Him with cleansed souls through the Eucharist, to walk in the light of His teaching in all that we do, to make Him our *real* and our *personal* Lord and Master in life. We refuse to pay a small price to receive a great gain. We are so wise in the things of the world and so ignorant in the things of the spirit. We thrill to the "big deal" we can make in business. But the greatest thing that can ever happen is when we come into possession of the riches of eternity through baptism and become joint heirs with Christ. It is this great treasure that the Church calls upon us to claim on the day of Epiphany by renewing our baptismal vows, by renouncing Satan and all of his works and accepting Christ as our Lord and Master.

Fr. Lev Gillet meditates on his reaffirmation of baptism on Epiphany when he writes:

> *"The water runs over me, and I see Thee in the Jordan, Lord, being baptized by John. Thou didst desire to receive that baptism not for Thyself, but for the sake of men. Thou didst receive John's baptism for my sake. Thou didst desire in all our names, in my name, as our representative and in place of us, to take repentance upon Thyself. It was the only moment of Thy life when Thou didst wish to appear a repentant sinner. For they were our sins which Thou didst bring to the imperfect baptism of John, anticipating the perfect baptism. I unite myself to Thee, in this baptism that Thou didst receive for me. And especially I unite myself to Thee so that through the strength of my desire there may be a renewal of that other baptism which I received from Thy disciples in Thy name, in the name of Thy Father, in the name of Thy Spirit. Thou Thyself, through human hands, baptized me. And it was into Thee that I was baptized."* [74]

The "Small and Great" Blessing

The Rite of the Blessing of Holy Water is celebrated on the Eve of the Feast as well as on the Feast Day itself. The first blessing was usually held in church and the second was often celebrated outdoors, on a lake or by a river or at the seashore. The custom of two blessings is explained by some to refer to the practice in the Early Church of blessing the water for the baptism of the catechumens on the Eve of the Feast, whereas on the day of the Feast itself the water was blessed for the sanctification of the faithful.

The two rites of blessing on Epiphany Eve and Epiphany are identical, though some have tried to introduce a distinction between the two through ill-informed piety. Another service, entirely different, called the Small Blessing of Water is used at other times during the year: the first of August, the feast of a patron saint, the Feast of Mid-Pentecost, as well as on other occasions. In the tradition of the Church it is customary to perform the Small Blessing of Water on the first day of each month.

During the first millenium of the Church, the blessing of water took place only once on the Eve of Epiphany. In fact, the typicons of the Studite Monastery and of Jerusalem prescribe only one blessing of water "since Christ was baptized only once not twice." The custom of blessing water twice: on the Eve as well as on the Feast of Epiphany dates from the eleventh century. It became a general practice in the thirteenth century. The reason for the double blessing was that the blessing on the Eve of the feast was regarded as a remembrance of the early practice of baptizing the catechumens, whereas the blessing on the Feast Day itself was celebrated in memory of Christ's baptism in the Jordan river. That is why the first blessing of water took place generally in the narthex of the church where the catechumens were formerly baptized, whereas the second blessing on Epiphany took place outside the sanctuary at some river, stream or well.

——— Holy Water Kept at Home the Year Round ———

It is customary to take holy water home and preserve it for use from time to time. St. John Chrysostom alluded to this practice when he wrote, "The faithful take water home and keep it throughout the year." Some bless themselves with it after confession, crossing their foreheads with it as a physical expression that the Master has cleansed His soiled disciple. Others bless themselves with it each morning. In the words of Fr. Lev Gillet: "When, each morning and during the day, I let water run over me, I can at the same time be washed, in spirit, by the water . . . of the Savior . . . Lord, behold, the water runs over me. I remember my sins. From my heart the words of the psalmist rise toward Thee: 'Wash me thoroughly from mine iniquity, and cleanse me from my sin. . . .' And I seem to hear Thy answer. . . . 'Come now . . . though your sins be as scarlet, they shall be made as white as snow. . . .' Oh, might I receive this assurance of salvation each morning, when I first wash myself."[75] Others keep the holy water at home in order to partake of it in time of illness or other personal or family needs.

Christmas and Epiphany in the Early Church

Almost until the end of the fourth century, most churches celebrated the Birth of Christ and His Baptism on the same day. The Feast was called Epiphany. The rationale behind this was that both feasts manifested Christ's divinity to the world. The birth of the Son manifested the Word made flesh, while His Baptism revealed God in Trinity.

It was during the lifetime of St. John Chrysostom that the two celebrations were separated in order to enforce the unique concept of each. In fact, in one of his sermons preached on Christmas Eve in 386, he mentions that only a few years before, in his very lifetime, both feasts were celebrated together. Chrysostom mentions as one of the reasons for the separation of the two feasts the fact that during His Baptism, Jesus was manifest to everyone, whereas at His Birth, He appeared in a hidden form. He writes, "It is not the day when Christ was born that should be called Epiphany, but the day when He was baptized. Not through His birth did He become known to all, but through His Baptism. Before the day of Baptism, He was not known to the people" (Orat. XV). Ever since that time, Christmas has been observed on December 25 and Epiphany on January 6. Today it is only the Armenian Church in the East that continues to celebrate the Nativity and Epiphany together on January 6. In the Western Church Epiphany has as its main objective the adoration of the Magi. In the East, the adoration of the Magi is celebrated together with Christmas on December 25.

The Dove as a Symbol

Vladimir Lossky writes concerning the symbolism of the dove at the Baptism of Jesus: "The holy Fathers of the Church explain the appearance of the Holy Spirit in the form of a dove at the Lord's Baptism by analogy with the Flood: just as then the world was purified of its iniquities by the waters of the Flood and the dove brought an olive branch into Noah's Ark, announcing the end of the Flood and peace returned upon the earth, so too now the Holy Spirit comes down in the form of a dove to announce the remission of sins and God's mercy to the world. 'There an olive branch, here the mercy of our God,' says St. John of Damascus."[76]

St. John Chrysostom said of the dove:

"Therefore the dove also appears not bearing an olive branch, but pointing out to us our Deliverer from all evils, and suggesting the gracious hopes. For not from out of an ark doth she lead one man only, but the whole world she leads up into heaven at her appearing, and instead of a branch of peace from an olive, she conveys the adoption to all the world's offspring in common."

We close with these beautiful words from the Rite of the Blessing of Water on Epiphany:

"*Magnify, O my soul, one of the Trinity who bowed
  his head and received baptism.
Today the Master buries in the waters the sin
  of mortal man.
Today the Master has come to sanctify the nature
  of the waters.
At thine appearing in the body,
The earth was sanctified,
The waters blessed,
The heaven enlightened,
And mankind set free from the bitter tyranny of
  the enemy.
O marvellous gifts! O divine grace, Forbearance
  past speech!
For see, the Creator and Master now wears
My nature in the Jordan, yet without sin;
He cleanses me through water,
Illumines me through fire,
And makes me perfect through the Holy Spirit.*

*The true Light has appeared,
And grants enlightenment to all.
Christ Who is above all purity is baptized with us;
He sanctifies the water
And it becomes a cleansing for our souls.
The outward sign is earthly,
The inward grace is higher than the heavens.
Salvation comes through washing,
And through water the Spirit:
Descending into the water we ascend to God.
Wonderful are thy works, O Lord: glory to thee.''*

FOOTNOTES . . .

[1] "The Orthodox Ethos" Edited by A. J. Philippou. Holywell Press. Oxford. 1964. p. 153.
[2] Avery Dulles, S.J., "The Symbolic Structure of Revelation," in "Theological Studies" 41 (1980) pp. 55-56.
[3] "A Sign For All Christians," W. Hardenbrook. Conciliar Press. P.O. Box 106. Mt. Hermon, CA 95041. © 1983. pp. 2-3.
[4] *"The First Day of Eternity"* George A. Maloney. Crossroad/New York. 1982. p. 90.
[5] "Institute for Ecumenical and Cultural Research" 1983. Collegeville, MN.
[6] "Interpreting Orthodoxy" N. Nissiotis. Light and Life Publ. Company/Mpls., MN. pp. 26, 27.
[7] "Orthodox Ethos" A. Philippou, Editor. Holywell Press. Oxford. 1964. p. 156.
[8] "All the Fullness of God" T. Hopko. SVS Press/Crestwood, NY. 1982. p. 39.
[9] "The Spiritual Counsels of Father John of Kronstadt." James Clarke Co., Ltd. London. 1967. p. 74.
[10] "Sacred Signs" by R. Guardini. Pio Decimo Press. St. Louis, MO. Copyright 1956. pp. 58, 59.
[11] "The Spiritual Counsels of Fr. John of Kronstadt" W. J. Grisbrooke. James Clarke Co. London. 1967. p. 90.
[12] "On the Song of Songs," Oration 10 (PG 44.985).
[13] Nilo Borgia, Il Commentario Liturgico Ji. S. Germano, Grottaferata 1912. p. 26.
[14] *"Treatise on Prayer"* St. Symeon of Thessalonika. Holy Cross Orthodox Press. Brookline, MA. 1984. p. 28.
[15] "Beyond East and West," Robert Taft, S.J., The Pastoral Press, Washington, D.C. © 1984. pp. 141-2.
[16] "The Spiritual Counsels of Fr. John of Kronstadt." Ed. W. J. Grisbrooke. James Clarke and Co., Ltd. London 1967. pp. 90-91.
[17] "Alone With the Alone," George A. Maloney. Ave Maria Press. Notre Dame, IN. © 1982. p. 173.
[18] "The Sayings of the Desert Fathers," Benedicta Ward. Mowbray Co., London. © 1975. p. 166.
[19] "The Art of Prayer" Chariton of Valamo. Faber and Faber. London. © 1966. P. 149 etc.
[20] "The Year of Grace of the Lord" by a Monk of the Eastern Church. SVS Press/Crestwood, NY. © 1980. p. 217.
[21] Taken from "Our Daily Walk," by F. B. Meyer. Used by permission of Zondervan Corp.
[22] "A Sign for All Christians" by W. Hardenbrook. Conciliar Press. P.O. Box 106. Mt. Hermon, CA 95041.
[23] "The Nicene Creed: Our Common Faith" E. Timiadis. Fortress Press. Philadelphia. 1983. p. 121.
[24] Taken from "Our Daily Walk," by F. B. Meyer. Used by permission of Zondervan Publishing Company.
[25] "Partakers of God" P. K. Chrestou. Holy Cross Orthodox Press. Brookline, MA. 1984. p. 64.
[26] Taken from "Our Daily Walk," by F. B. Meyer. Used by permission of Zondervan Publishing Company.
[27] "Ladder of Divine Ascent" Translated by Lazarus Moore. Faber and Faber.

Copyright 1959. p. 19.

[28] "Ladder of Divine Ascent" Translated by Lazarus Moore. Faber and Faber. Copyright 1959. p. 19.

[29] "The Way of the Heart" Nouwen. The Seabury Press. New York. Copyright 1981. p. 82.

[30] "Sacred Signs," R. Guardini. Pio Decimo Press: St. Louis, MO. Copyright 1956. p. 35.

[31] "Ladder of Divine Ascent" Translated by Lazarus Moore. Faber and Faber: London. Copyright 1959. p. 32.

[32] Kallistos Ware, "The Power of the Name." SLG Press, Fairacres, Oxford.

[33] N. Cabasilas, *De Vita in Christo* 6; PG 150; 657-659.

[34] G. Winckler, "Prayer Attitude in the Eastern Church." Light and Life Publishing Company. Minneapolis, MN.

[35] "The Way of the Heart," H. Nouwen. Seabury Press: New York. 1981. p. 30.

[36] "The Time of the Spirit," George Every, Richard Harries, Kallistos Ware. SVS Press. 1984. SVS Press. Crestwood, NY. p. 210.

[37] "The Way of the Heart," H. Nouwen. Seabury Press: New York. 1981. pp. 27, 28, 32.

[38] St. Gregory Palamas and Orthodox Spirituality." John Meyendorff. SVS Press: Scarsdale, NY. 1974. p. 113.

[39] "The Ladder of Divine Ascent" Translated by Lazarus Moore. Faber and Faber: London. 1957. p. 71.

[40] *O Holy Mountain* Basil Pennington. Doubleday and Company: New York. 1978. p. 64.

[41] "Growing Spiritually" E. S. Jones Abingdon Press, Nashville, TN. Copyright 1953. p. 69.

[42] From an Ashram message: "What Happens to Self?" United Christian Ashrams. Barrington, Rhode Island.

[43] "The Orthodox Church" by Kallistos Ware (pp. 232-233). Viking-Penguin, New York, NY.

[44] SOBORNOST Vol. 7. Number 1. 1985. "Rejoice, Sceptre of Orthodoxy" by Elizabeth Briere. p. 21.

[45] "The Year of Grace of the Lord" by a Monk of the Eastern Church. SVS Press/Crestwood, NY. Copyright 1980. p. 90.

[46] "Nea Estia," Athens, 1955, Christmas issue, pp. 408-409.

[47] *St. Augustine, "On Holy Virginity" 3 (PL 40, 398): Sermon 215, No. 4 (PL 38, 1074).*

[48] "The Nicene Creed: Our Common Faith," E. Timiadis. Fortress Press/Philadelphia. © 1983. p. 75.

[49] "Jesus Christ — the Life of the World." Edited by I. Bria. WCC/Geneva. © 1982. p. 85.

[50] "Byzantine Theology," John Meyendorff. Forham University Press/NY. © 1974. p. 115.

[51] "The Good Shepherd," Lesslie Newbigin. Wm . C. Eerdmans/Grand Rapids. © 1977. p. 37.

[52] "The Spiritual Counsels of Father John of Kronstadt," Edited by W. J. Grisbrooke. J. Clarke and Company/London. © 1967. p. 42.

[53] "Introduction to Liturgical Theology," A. Schmemann. The Faith Press/London. © 1966. p. 13.

[54] "For the Life of the World," A. Schmemann. National Student Christian Federation/NY. 1963. pp. 13, 16.

[55] "Religion in Communist Lands," No. 2, 1974. pp. 24-25.
[56] "For the Life of the World," A. Schmemann. Ibid. p. 30.
[57] "The Melody of Prayer," S. Harakas. Light and Life Publishing/Minneapolis, MN. 1979. pp. 21-24.
[58] Sobornost. Vol. 7. Number, 1985. "Liturgy and Eschatology" by A. Schmemann. pp. 10-11.
[59] "For the Life of the World," A. Schmemann. Nat'l Christian Student Fed./NY. 1966. p. 16.
[60] "The Nicene Creed: Our Common Faith," E. Timiadis. Fortress Press/Philadelphia. 1983. p. 57.
[61] *"For the Life of the World,"* A. Schmemann. Nat'l Student Christian Federation. (NY 1963). pp. 29-30.
[62] "The Sermon and the Liturgy," GOTR. Vol. 28, Number 4. Winter 1983.
[63] "Give Me One Good Reason Why I Should Go To Church." Conciliar Press, Box 106, Mt. Hermon, CA 95041.
[64] "Clergy and Laity in the Church," SVS Press, Crestwood, NY. p. 10.
[65] "Worship," T. Hopko. Dept. Rel. Education — OCA. Syosett, NY. Copyright 1972. P. 62.
[66] "The Faith We Hold," Archbishop Paul of Finland. SVS Press/Crestwood, NY. 1980. p. 48.
[67] K. Kirchoff, "Das heilige Jahr," in "Der Christliche Osten," 1939. p. 93.
[68] "The Winter Pascha," Fr. Thomas Hopko. SVS Press. Crestwood, NY. Copyright 1984. pp. 149, etc. SVS Press, Crestwood, NY. p. 210.
[69] "The Festal Menaion" by Mother Mary and Bishop Kallistos Ware. Faber and Faber/London. © 1969. p. 58.
[70] "Orthodox Spirituality," by a Monk of the Eastern Church. S.P.C.K./London. 1968. p. 41.
[71] "The Festal Menaion." Faber and Faber. London. 1969. p. 56.
[72] St. Vladimir's Seminary Press. Crestwood, NY.
[73] "The Festal Menaion" by Mother Mary and Kallistos Ware. Faber and Faber. London. 1969. p. 58.
[74] "In Thy Presence," Lev. Gillet. SVS Press. Crestwood, NY. 1977. p. 86.
[75] "In Thy Presence," Fr. Lev. Gillet. St. Vladimir's Seminary Press. Crestwood, NY. 1977. pp. 85, 87.
[76] "The Meaning of Icons," L. Ouspensky and V. Lossky. Boston Book and Art Shop. 1952. p. 167.